BAYLEY 4 CLINICAL USE AND INTERPRETATION

Practical Resources for the Mental Health Professional

BAYLEY 4 CLINICAL USE AND INTERPRETATION

GLEN P. AYLWARD
Professor Emeritus, Pediatrics and Psychiatry
Southern Illinois University School of Medicine
Springfield, IL, United States

Academic Press is an imprint of Elsevier
125 London Wall, London EC2Y 5AS, United Kingdom
525 B Street, Suite 1650, San Diego, CA 92101, United States
50 Hampshire Street, 5th Floor, Cambridge, MA 02139, United States
The Boulevard, Langford Lane, Kidlington, Oxford OX5 1GB, United Kingdom

Library of Congress Cataloging-in-Publication Data
A catalog record for this book is available from the Library of Congress

British Library Cataloguing-in-Publication Data
A catalogue record for this book is available from the British Library

ISBN: 978-0-12-817754-9

For information on all Academic Press publications
visit our website at https://www.elsevier.com/books-and-journals

Publisher: Nikki Levy
Editorial Project Manager: Barbara Makinster
Production Project Manager: Kiruthika Govindaraju
Cover Designer: Mark Rogers

Typeset by SPi Global, India

Contents

Foreword

In so many ways, Glen P. Aylward is the perfect person to assume the legacy of Nancy Bayley and become the author of the Bayley-4. Since her passing, professional staff of The Psychological Corporation (later known as Harcourt Assessment and eventually Pearson Clinical Assessment) have become the stewards of her legacy and guided the development of Bayley-II and Bayley-III. Several people at the publishing company contributed greatly to the Bayley-II and Bayley-III without the benefit of Dr. Bayley's guidance. Dr. Jim Gurkye improved the psychometric quality of the Bayley-II by ensuring a well-stratified normative sample and improving the reliability of measurement. Dr. Aurelio Prifitera was the first to envision the expansion of the Bayley-III to include adaptive functioning and social-emotional development, and Dr. Kathleen Matula further improved the psychometric soundness of the test. Under the stewardship of the publisher's staff, the Bayley evolved from a useful clinical tool to perhaps the most psychometrically sound scientific instruments for the assessment of infants and toddlers. However, it also increased in length and complexity, becoming somewhat grueling for both examiners and examinees.

As Vice President of Global Research & Development for Pearson Clinical Assessment (now retired), I felt that the Bayley-III was as psychometrically sound as possible, and the touch of a master clinician was once again needed to take Bayley-4 to the next level. Dr. Aylward's name came to mind as the natural choice as he had been on the publisher's advisory panel for the previous two editions, was the author of the Bayley Infant Neurodevelopmental Screener, and an internationally respected scholar as well as a masterful clinician. I flew to Springfield Illinois and spent 2 days peppering Glen with questions about how he would improve the test. We debated dozens of difficult topics such as how to make adjustments for prematurity and the implications of including at-risk infants in the normative sample on the precision of diagnostic cut scores. But, my mind was made up the second he said, "If I could become the author of the next Bayley-I would consider it the capstone of my career." At that moment, I knew that he not only had all the right answers to my clinical and research questions, but also an inner passion for the Bayley that was unmatched. Then he put the icing on the cake saying that his overarching goal was to make the

Bayley "easier to use and more clinically informative." He has exceeded every expectation with Bayley-4.

Dr. Aylward's unique contributions to Bayley-4 are many. He has provided us with a contemporary theoretical foundation for the instrument based on a sound synthesis of neurological and environmental perspective that is well-articulated in Chapter 1—which should require reading by all Bayley-4 users. Here he discusses the role of neural plasticity and canalization and epigenetics providing an integration of environmental issues with cognitive theory, attachment theory, and maturational theory, including an enlightening discussion of critical and sensitive periods of development. He has made the test easier to administer by allowing care-giver report if the baby is uncooperative on some items, reducing administration times, and collaborating with the publishers' technology staff to create a portable digital tool that helps practitioners structure the administration while allowing them flexibility to jump around in the item sequence and record spontaneously observed behaviors. From a clinical perspective, he has pioneered a new polytomous scoring system that allows practitioners to differentiate emerging from mastered behaviors, added more low-functioning items, and provided a new autism spectrum checklist. Finally, he has improved the diagnostic sensitivity of the scores by collecting a typically functioning normative sample whose mean scores are unsuppressed by inclusion of at-risk subjects, thus making it easier to identify delay.

Dr. Aylward is an Associate Editor of the Journal of Developmental and Behavioral Pediatrics and Director of the NICU Follow-up program. But, those who know Glen personally are aware of his witty and dry sense of humor, which comes out briefly in the first part of his preface. He is full of funny stories of things kids do during testing and hearing him present live would be a real treat for anyone.

The consummate scientist-practitioner, Dr. Aylward, has succeeded in his goal of making the Bayley-4 easier to use and more clinically informative and his passion for the instrument shines through at every turn.

Lawrence G. Weiss

Introduction

I am honored to be the author of the Bayley-4 and to carry on the tradition set forth by Nancy Bayley of providing the reference standard for infant and toddler assessment. First, to dispel a rumor circulating as to why I was selected to author the new test, let me clarify that I am *not* related to Nancy Bayley. However, I did meet her once many years ago in Denver, Colorado, when I was a graduate student attending SRCD. I seriously doubt that I made much of an impression at that time, although she was very cordial. I also saw her original notes on the Bayley when I was working on the Bayley Infant Neurodevelopmental Screener at Psych Corp in San Antonio in the early 1990s. I perceived that she was very detail-oriented as evident by the numerous pages dedicated to selecting the proper size for the blocks to be used with the test.

I am also in possession of an exclusive "un-decapitated" doll that was used in the "broken doll" series on the original Bayley. Arguably, this may or may not be an additional, legitimate reason for my selection as an author. All the little figures were produced with their heads attached, but they were routinely decapitated with a box-cutter by one of the warehouse personnel before shipping. I guess I have a rescue doll, as I retrieved one before it met its gruesome fate with the box-cutter. To put the doll in context, it was introduced by giving the child the body and head and the examiner then saying "this is broken, fix it" or "mend it" or "make it good again."The child could reattach the head "marginally,""approximately," or "exactly." Needless to say, some placements were rather "unique." Incidentally, by popular consensus, this item was not included in any subsequent edition of the Bayley (thereby leaving the warehouse guy with the box-cutter in search of new employment).

Further underscoring my qualifications to author the Bayley-4, I have the unique distinction of administering the original Bayley to a Siamang-Gibbon hybrid from the Atlanta zoo who was placed in the Georgia State University "monkey lab." Dr. Duane Rumbaugh, the department chair, and other monkey lab folks thought it would be great sport to see how a primate would fare on the Bayley. Possessing a bit of Bayley braggadocio, I readily accepted the challenge and administered the test to the little ape who was about 6 or so months old and named something like Kisu Kisu (I believe it meant "kiss-kiss" in Japanese). Knowing very little Japanese, I had absolutely nothing to do with the name and Dr. Rumbaugh disavowed any involvement as well. The Siamang/Gibbon hybrid (I later found out when Google came along that there are 10 other types of Gibbons besides the Siamang, which is the largest) scored at a level approximately 6 months higher than the average human would at her age, adding credibility to sequels of Planet of the Apes.

On a more serious note, I have been working with children for more than 45 years and began my work with infants at Grady Memorial Hospital in Atlanta in 1974. I worked in the NICU administering the Prechtl Newborn Neurological examination and revised it for preterm infants. I also administered the Bayley in the follow-up clinic. My interests in neurology were further nurtured by Emory faculty in neurology and neonatology: Drs. Jim Schwartz, Peter Ahman, Bill Kanto, and my mentor, Al Brann. Other influential developmental and high-risk infant specialists included Arthur Parmelee, M.D., Josephine Brown, Ph.D., Anneliese Korner, Ph.D., and many others.

My big break came when I became involved with the NIH-NHLBI Dexamethasone study where I participated in the follow-up aspects of this RCT on the effect of prenatal steroids on lung maturation. The Bayley was an integral measure at 9 and 18-months and the McCarthy Scales were given at age 3 years. I used data from the follow-up to develop the Early Neuropsychologic Optimality Rating Scales (ENORS), which, with encouragement from Jim Gyrke, Ph.D., and Kathleen Matula, Ph.D., from Psych Corp, eventually morphed into the Bayley Infant Neurodevelopmental Screener (BINS; Aylward, 1995). In addition, I have participated on the Advisory Boards of the Bayley-II and Bayley-III.

Over the many years evaluating infants, problematic issues tended to surface repeatedly: Tests were too darn long; most infants were not up to doing what a stranger said for 90 minutes at a clip; infants typically had their own test agendas which did not follow the rigid administration rules spelled out in test manuals; being a psychometrician or psychologist did not automatically qualify the person as an expert with regard to infant testing; some items and concepts were flat-out odd (e.g., the headless doll); and finally, there were strong experiential biases at work (the infant's performance being influenced by their previous experiences with similar test components). This last issue was driven home many years ago by an experience in our follow-up clinic with a 2½-year-old child from poor environmental circumstances. When given the blocks that Dr. Bayley had worked so diligently to select, he held two in his fisted hand, blew on them, shook his hand, mumbled something, and rolled them on the table acting quite excited as they rolled (much to the chagrin of his embarrassed caregiver). Obviously, his pretesting experience had an impact on his performance. Exposure to items used in test tasks (e.g., pegs, scissors, form boards) and training to task in intervention programs still confound the validity of many of these measures.

Many questions were also raised and still persist today: what is the relationship between early, simple behaviors, and later cognitive skills; what factors affect brain development which then is evident in performance on developmental tests; instead of identifying deficits, could items be identified that are optimal and predictive of positive scores; how big of a role should parents play in developmental assessment, and, as a corollary, what factors affect parent report? Some of these are addressed in the Bayley-4.

I am grateful to Psych Corp and Pearson for the opportunity to author the Bayley-4, particularly Larry Weiss and Cheryl McDougald, for selecting me and having faith that I could pull this off!

Finally, I would like to thank my wife, Deborah, for her encouragement and tolerating me holed up in my office for long periods of time, and my children, Shawn, Megan, Brandon, and Mason, and my five grandchildren for providing me with an extended practicum on child development.

Glen P. Aylward

CHAPTER 1

Brain, environment, and development: A synthesis and a conceptual model

Contents

Bayley 4 Clinical Use and Interpretation
https://doi.org/10.1016/B978-0-12-817754-9.00001-5

Introduction

This chapter contains an overview of several pertinent processes that affect brain development and developmental assessment. These include the concepts of neuronal plasticity, environmental influences, and epigenetics. An overarching theme is that environmental input will affect brain neuro- and synaptogenesis. These effects, in turn, will have an impact on the infant and toddler's cognitive, language, motor, and social development, as well as our ability to assess these constructs. Application of this approach to other theories and discussion of the negative effects of brain alternations due to disruption and/or insult are also addressed.

Multiple, rapid changes in brain functions that underlie behavioral development occur in infancy and toddlerhood. These changes include development of higher-order capacities such as attention, working memory, and self-regulation—also known as executive functions (EFs; Guyer, Perez-Edgar, & Crone, 2018).

Changes from earlier theoretic orientations

The previous Bayley Scales (Bayley, 1969, 1993, 2006) were developed without subscribing to a specific theory of child development. However, the Bayley-4 is influenced by evolving concepts and new data regarding factors that affect brain function and related early developmental acquisitions. Essentially, this is an integrated *neuro-environmental synthesis model* of development. Basically, *external* biological and environmental influences work in combination to affect the course of *internal* brain development (Shonkoff & Gardner, 2012). In turn, brain changes are assumed to be manifest in behaviors that can be observed or assessed with instruments such as the Bayley-4. Stated differently, the child's central nervous system (CNS) undergoes biological maturation, with changes in structure and function occurring in response to experience and/or injury. This, in turn, influences the dynamics of synaptic connections and formation of neural circuits, leading to developmental gains and increased complexity in behavior.

Biological components of development include brain growth and plasticity (e.g., synaptogenesis, myelination, and pruning), as well as epigenetic modifications (methylation, microRNAs, histone modification) that will be discussed subsequently. Brain growth involves *additions* such as creating new connections, as well as *deletions* (pruning).

Environment can exert negative effects via physical exposures (e.g., tobacco, Bisphenol A, lead, alcohol, and other toxicants), experiences (e.g., NICU experiences that overwhelm the infant's immature nervous system with nociceptive, visual, auditory, and proprioceptive sensory input), and social transactions (early life adversity, abuse/neglect, low SES, lack of stimulation, poor quality caregiver-child interaction, and allostatic load). Environmental components affecting brain development are classified as: (a) events of *omission*, where factors that are necessary for normal brain development are absent (e.g., the preterm infant does not receive intrauterine nutrients critical for third trimester brain development); and (b) events of *commission* where adverse effects to the brain are caused by exposure to substances that should not be present (e.g., fetal alcohol, Bisphenol A) (Georgieff, Tran, & Carlson, 2018). The omissions and commissions can also work in combination as in the case of fetal alcohol exposure (commission) that leads to iron deficiency (omission). (Georgieff et al., 2018).

Recent data indicate that children living 1.5 times below federal poverty level have smaller brain volumes in brain regions critical for cognitive and academic performance, namely gray matter, frontal and temporal lobes, and the hippocampus (Noble et al., 2015). This again underscores an environmental influence on brain development. Nutrition, inflammatory processes, and intrauterine exposures also must be considered. There is growing awareness that negative experiences or exposures do not have to be extreme to have an impact (i.e., not necessarily total deprivation or excessive stimulation), and seemingly innocuous exposures can still have significant effects on brain development (Kolb, Harker, & Gibb, 2017).

In the case of synaptogenesis and pruning (which provide the basis for central nervous system plasticity and functional capabilities), *the brain* responds or "listens" to the environment. In epigenetics, however, *genes* respond to the environment.

Canalization

Canalization, conceptualized as prewired, species-specific neural circuits that facilitate simple behaviors, also plays a significant role in early development (McCall, 1983). Canalized behaviors are primarily sensorimotor and tend to be resistant to negative influences such as perinatal trauma, prematurity, or hypoxic ischemic encephalopathy, provided these negative influences are not severe. Canalized behaviors are relatively simple (e.g., smiling, reaching, babbling), self-righting, and are in contrast to increasingly complex higher-order functions that are more susceptible to disruption. The canalized behaviors are buffered so that minor perturbations can be compensated for without causing a major developmental problem (Johnson, Jones, & Gliga, 2015).

Early infant tests typically are heavily weighted with tasks involving canalized behaviors; this may partially explain why predicting later outcome is so difficult, because later higher-order functions require more complex and vulnerable circuits that are not functional early on.

During development, brain alterations range from the cellular level (e.g., dendritic organization) to synaptic structuring, to changes in functional organization. These brain changes, particularly growth of new synapses and neural networks, are inferred to be the source of behavioral changes that are assessed in developmental evaluation. Although a direct linkage between brain changes and observable behavior is assumed, in actuality we are faced with associations that are not clearly causative or necessarily fixed over time (Kolb & Gibb, 2013).

Neuronal plasticity

Types of neural circuits

Neuronal plasticity in typical development refers to structural and functional changes in neuronal circuits that are in response to experience (Fu & Zuo, 2011). Plasticity is associated with increased capacity for learning. There are three types of neural circuits that are involved in plasticity: (1) *experience-independent*; (2) *experience-expectant*; and (3) *experience-dependent* (Greenough, Black, & Wallace, 1987). Experience-independent synapses (largely a prenatal process) are groupings of cells that are connected and fire together in response to internal stimulation. This repeated synchrony in firing in the absence of external sensory input further strengthens connections of the cells within the group and refines brain connectivity. Cell assemblies that fire out of synch gradually weaken and become nonfunctional (e.g., Campbell & Shatz, 1992).

Experience-expectant synapses are innate and prewired, but to become functional, they need to receive input (essentially being activity-dependent). Input occurs mostly during early postnatal development (Kolb et al., 2017). For example, prior to 6 months of age, infants are "wired" to discriminate phonemes in all languages. At approximately 6–10 months, this ability diminishes, while the infant's ability to discriminate phonemes in the native language to which he or she is exposed increases (Kuhl, Williams, Lacerda, Stevens, & Lindblom, 1992). Babbling provides another experience-expectant example: Initially, infants babble all sounds of a language, but this becomes restricted to the sounds heard repeatedly in the environment. Even children who are deaf babble initially, but without environmental input, this behavior is extinguished. Stated differently, anticipatory circuits that are stimulated or primed by external input become stronger and increasingly functional, while those without adequate stimulation do not. Fine-tuning networks in response to repetitive input enhance precision and then provide a basis for *integration* of separate networks—this is considered to be the foundation of higher-order processing (Blair & Raver, 2012).

Experience-dependent synapses can be modified in response to environmental experiences and account for learning and memory formation (Greenough & Chang, 1989). Existing neuronal assemblies (these are not "prewired") are changed by these experiences, thereby increasing or decreasing the number of synapses in different brain areas (Kolb & Gibb, 2013). Early interventions may enhance the development of these experience-dependent synapses, while lack of stimulation can lead to nonbeneficial pruning. New learning involves development of synaptic networks that are dynamic and become more complex over time.

Critical and sensitive periods

Depending on timing, certain brain areas are more responsive to environmental influences than others (Guyer et al., 2018). Pruning and synaptogenesis also suggest that neural networks are malleable during early development, and early childhood experience-dependent plasticity underscores both the relatively high vulnerability and the adaptability of the developing brain (Luby, 2015). Age has a major effect on the degree of plasticity and synaptogenesis, making the stage of brain development at the time of exposure to a negative environmental or biological event a key factor in the reorganizational response (Fiori & Guzzetta, 2015). A series of time-dependent, critical or sensitive windows is contained in the preprogrammed maturational blueprint of brain development (Nemati & Kolb, 2012). In critical periods, a genetic pattern of connectivity is consolidated by exposure to specific input—absence of that input leads to abnormal connections. These "critical periods" are defined as a time when neuronal connections are highly susceptible to experience-expectant and experience-dependent modifications (Hensch, 2004; Kolb et al., 2017). This was exquisitely demonstrated in Hubel and Weisel's early work involving the plasticity of cat and monkey visual systems (Hubel & Wiesel, 1970). These investigators found that deprivation of input at certain times can irreversibly change neural connections and functions. Duration of exposure to the adverse event during the critical period is important—if the adversity is terminated before the critical period is over, there exists a chance for partial recovery (Georgieff et al., 2018).

In contrast, sensitive periods are more flexible, with neural circuits having multiple, genetically programmed connection patterns that can be selected, depending on external input. Stated differently, critical periods are more rigid with regard to timing; sensitive periods are more flexible to a degree. All critical periods are sensitive periods, but the reverse is not true (Knudsen, 2004).

Neural systems have different sensitive periods and plasticity is greatest during these times (Johnson, Riis, & Noble, 2016). Hence, there are critical windows of time where the brain is able to reorganize and other times where it cannot; this has significant ramifications in regard to vulnerability to negative environmental factors and the ability to recover from injury (Kolb, Mychasiuk, Williams, & Gibb, 2011). Also, the more specialized an integrated neural network becomes, the less plasticity it possesses (Johnson et al., 2015).

Summary of plasticity

Functional, integrated neural circuits that underlie development are sculpted from a pool of less specific and less defined synaptic groupings. Experience modifies these connections via the processes of enhancement or elimination. The child initially possesses excessive synaptic connections; experiential input determines which survive and which are eliminated (via the mechanism of apoptosis or pruning). Brain development, therefore, is intimately related to environmental input that could be positive or negative. Environmental and sensory Input is needed to strengthen prewired networks and enhance development of new interconnections. Similarly, lack of input weakens synapses. These interconnections vary in terms of permanency, making development nonlinear. Moreover, changes vary in terms of long-term persistence. Positive early life experiences can perhaps reverse some of the effects of negative influences, most likely via experience-expectant mechanisms (Miguel, Pereira, Silveira, & Meany, 2019).

Major changes in brain development occur in utero and continue over the first 2 years (Casey, Giedd, & Thomas, 2000). Increased cognitive capacity during childhood may actually coincide with a *loss* of existing synapses, versus formation of new ones. Synaptic density peaks at different ages in specific areas of the brain (e.g., the auditory cortex at 3 months, the middle frontal gyrus at 15 months). The dorsolateral prefrontal cortex is the last brain region to mature (Casey et al., 2000). Brain regions that are most malleable over prolonged developmental periods also are susceptible to negative environmental factors such as stressors or toxicants during this time as well (Casey et al., 2000).

An intriguing corollary is the concept of *neural reuse* (Anderson, 2016). This is defined as a process whereby neural circuits developed for one role are also conscripted for other subsequent uses. Stated differently, localized specialization of function may be the exception rather than the rule; learning not only involves fine-tuning local connections between cells, but also the development of long-distance interconnections. Local brain regions support diverse tasks across cognitive domains and the mix of tasks that each supports differs by region. The two most important developmental features of neural reuse plasticity are: (1) brain regions that develop early subsequently are used in more diverse functions because they are available for reuse longer; and (2) cognitive functions developed later employ more widely scattered brain regions because fewer local circuits are available. Thus, there is less reason to believe that functional circuits would be anatomically close together in the brain (Anderson, 2010).

Application to developmental assessment

In the neuro-environmental synthesis orientation, development is viewed as dynamic and our ability to assess an infant's behavioral acquisitions varies. For example, the term, *experiential bias*, is mentioned in the Bayley-4 manual (Bayley & Aylward, 2019a, 2019b). This reflects the possibility that inexperience with certain test components such as scissors, which results in poor performance on tasks involving cutting, does not necessarily reflect a deficit in fine-motor function. Rather, it may be the result of lack of exposure to scissors that results underdeveloped experience-dependent neural circuits needed for this function. Experience-dependent networks are unique to each child because of different interactions with the environment (Greenough et al., 1987). In fact, if the child who was unacquainted with scissors had experience with other test components such as blocks and could perform these tasks well, this would discount the likelihood of a fine-motor deficit.

These findings have provided the impetus for the change in scoring on the Bayley-4. Rather than a dichotomous, 0 or 1 scoring format, consideration was given to the rate of emergence of a particular skill. If an infant does not display mastery, but does show an approximation of the skill, this may be due to a lack of experience or practice, and the assumed underdeveloped experience-dependent circuits. Nonetheless, the basics are extant. With continued exposure and strengthening of these experience-dependent synaptic assemblies, the skill will be mastered. This differs from the child who does not display any approximation of the behavior whatsoever. In this case, subsequent functional synaptogenesis or development of efficient circuits required to accomplish the behavior is more questionable.

To reiterate, cognition is hypothesized to be the result of orchestrated information flow between neurons across extended white matter pathways, versus processes restricted to certain areas of the brain (Keunen et al., 2017). There is a relationship between path length (which is assumed to be a measure of brain network efficiency) and intelligence (particularly with performance IQ) (Keunen et al., 2017). Stated differently, higher-order cognitive functions involve more complex and geographically distant brain circuits and increased complexity and distance make these circuits more susceptible to insult. Because the circuits develop later, it is difficult to predict subsequent cognitive abilities from early infant tests.

Epigenetics

Epigenetics is a hot topic and also affects brain development and subsequent behavior, but in a different fashion. Epigenetics means "above" or "over" genetics and involves gene × environment molecular processes that affect development (Lester, Conradt, & Marsit, 2016). Epigenetics is also considered to be a key factor in brain growth and development (Dan, 2017), although the dynamics differ from brain plasticity (Nigg, 2018). With epigenetics, environment again plays a part in the child's experiences, affecting the *activity* of DNA without changing the DNA itself.

Components of epigenetics

Cells contain chromosomes that are composed of strands of DNA that hold genes. In the genes, DNA has genetic information that is stored as a code (Lester et al., 2016). The DNA code produces an exact copy of itself transcribed in RNA, which, in turn, is translated and produces proteins that determine the structure and function of the individual cell. In humans, DNA methylation is the most studied epigenetic mechanism. Levels of methylation (turning genes on and off) regulate or determine how well the DNA is transcribed into RNA, which, in turn, is translated into proteins that contribute to the brain's architecture. Increased methylation (i.e., turning off the gene transcription) corresponds to decreases in transcription until the gene is totally switched off and proteins are not produced. However, methylation is not simply analogous to an "on/off" switch, but instead resembles a rheostat. As a result, there are gradations of methylation.

Other components of epigenetics include microRNAs (molecules that act as posttranscriptional regulators of gene expression) and histone modifications (involve how molecules attach to proteins and alter the activity of the DNA wrapped around them). These components will not be discussed in detail.

The key epigenetic concepts are outlined in the following figure:

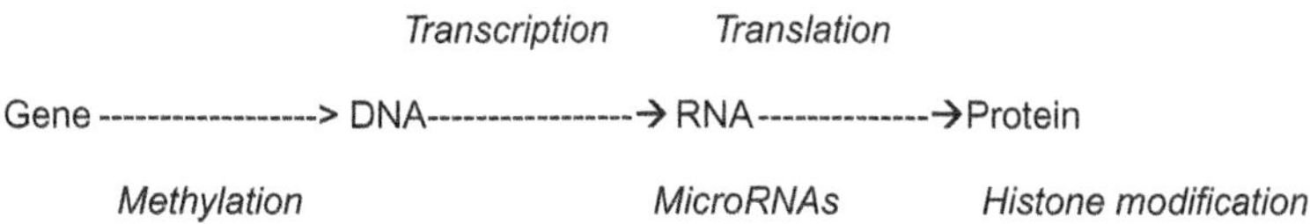

Basically, epigenetic mechanisms control *how the gene is expressed*. Epigenetics mediates relations between biological and environmental factors and how these relations affect child development. Structures and functions can be reprogrammed, producing a different type of brain plasticity. The process is dynamic and enables a variety of phenotypes to develop from the same genotype, depending on environmental factors (Lester, Marsit, Conradt, Bromer, & Padbury, 2012; Lester et al., 2016).

For example, glucocorticoid receptors and resultant levels of circulating cortisol are negatively affected by maternal smoking (Knopik, Maccani, Francazio, & McGeary, 2012) as is the expression of brain regulatory genes instrumental in brain growth, myelination, and neuronal migration. Early prenatal or postnatal adversity also has a negative effect on glucocorticoid receptors and the structure and function of the amygdala and hippocampus (Parade et al., 2016; Romens, Mc Donald, Svaren, & Pollak, 2015). This has an impact on the neuroendocrine reaction to stress and internalizing behavior problems. These experiences can be prenatal and postnatal. The serotonin gene is sensitive to variations in postnatal maternal care and increased methylation attributed to poor postnatal M-I interactions is associated with infant temperament problems (Champagne & Curley, 2009). Orphanage rearing is associated with diminished autonomic hypothalamic-pituitary-adrenal neuraxis function and changes in the amygdala. Similarly, the oxytocin receptor is affected by abuse in childhood (Smearman et al., 2016), with a resultant impact on later socialization (assessed by the Social/Emotional Scale of the Bayley-4).

The main point is that epigenetics has a major impact on brain growth which is then manifest in observable behavior and testable developmental acquisitions. Methylation affects brain development in terms of neuronal plasticity, cell proliferation, and apoptosis. Epigenetic mechanisms regulate the expression of genes involved in learning and memory via finely tuned, nuanced expression and silencing of genes. In the extreme, these mechanisms also are associated with neurodevelopmental disorders such as Rett Syndrome, Fragile X, Angelman's Syndrome, and Prader-Willi (Dan, 2017).

Environment

Environmental studies have documented a relationship between child poverty and brain structure (Johnson et al., 2016). Brain areas involved in memory, emotional regulation, and higher-order cognitive functioning are particularly susceptible (i.e., hippocampus, amygdala, and prefrontal cortex). Moreover, the cortical areas of the left hemisphere responsible for language and literacy skills are also affected. Child poverty affects the brain at the molecular, neural, cognitive, and behavioral levels early on because the brain has an exceptional growth rate from late gestation up to 2 years. The number of synapses peaks in the first few years, plateaus, and then declines in later childhood (Lenroot & Giedd, 2006).

Components of the environment

The child's environment contains "process" components (proximal aspects experienced most directly by the child such as mother-infant interactions, opportunities for stimulation in the home) as well as "status" features (distal, more broad components experienced indirectly such as SES or the child's neighborhood) (Aylward, 1992, 2010). Process features generally are more influential early on, particularly during the age range of the Bayley-4. Status factors are more influential in later childhood or adolescence (Brooks-Gunn, Duncan, & Aber, 1997).

Therefore, there is an evolving proximal-distal locus of environmental influence where the magnitude of qualitative effects on development from different environment components changes over time. Environmental exposures are additive and unfavorable environmental characteristics tend to cluster. The influence of different environmental characteristics is age-specific: experiences that are in play closer to time of assessment will be most influential. This interplay of variables is dynamic and not fixed over time (Aylward, 2010).

Extrapolation to other theories and developmental assessment

To reiterate, both plasticity and epigenetics have a substantial impact on brain development. At any given testing period, plasticity and epigenetics theoretically contribute in different degrees. For example, early in development, canalized networks would drive the infant's responses, although pre-, peri-, and postnatal biological and environmental factors could alter these behaviors via epigenetic processes. In parallel, the role of experience-expectant circuits intensifies. As developmental tasks become more complex and require learning new skills, the importance of experience-dependent synaptogenesis increases dramatically.

Cognitive theory

This synthesis can explain certain components of extant developmental theories. For example, drawing from Piaget's work (Piaget & Inhelder, 1969), these brain changes and environmental exposures could underlie the core concepts of *assimilation* and *accommodation*. The former involves taking information in and fitting it to preexisting cognitive structures; the latter entails adjustment or modification of existing cognitive structures to understand information or deal with new challenges—i.e., plasticity. Piaget considered these mental structures or circuits to be *schemata*. Experience-dependent synapses would have a prominent role (i.e., in learning), as would earlier experience-expectant circuits (sensorimotor development), both of which are affected by environment. This balance of assimilation and accommodation creates a state of equilibrium that lasts until something novel is experienced in the environment which requires the child to develop a new schema by intrinsically "experimenting" with the environment. This produces new integrated neural networks and accounts for learning. Because these are considered precursors of later intelligence, it is recommended that developmental assessment should include measurement of these abilities.

Attachment theory

With regard to Spitz's and Bowlby's (Bowlby & King, 2004) work in attachment theory, relationships with primary caregivers may have neuroanatomic effects by triggering reorganization and fine-tuning of synaptic circuits, particularly the prefrontal-limbic connections (Braun & Bock, 2011). Depending on the intensity, duration, nature, and complexity of the early environment, social deprivation may induce negative synaptic adaptations and different genetic expression (via epigenetics). When the child is later exposed to a more "normal" social-emotional experience, the previously adaptive synapses and pathways and their associated behaviors may now be maladaptive and cause an inability to process the new input, resulting in the child displaying abnormal behaviors (Braun & Bock, 2011). This type of function is measured by the Social-Emotional scale of the Bayley-4.

Maturational theory

Plasticity and epigenetics can also be applied to Maturational theory (Gesell, 1945). In the maturational approach, development is determined primarily by internal factors that are controlled by genes. Developmental change is assumed to be based solely on a maturational blueprint; the actual sequence is invariant, but the rate is variable.

Amiel-Tison and Gosselin (2008) also adopt a maturational approach in the conceptualization of lower and upper motor control systems. The lower system involves the brainstem and cerebellum and matures by 24-weeks gestation. It controls posture against gravity, flexor tone in the limbs, and primitive reflexes. The upper system is comprised of the cerebral hemispheres and basal ganglia, matures later (32 weeks), and exerts control over the lower system via relaxation of limbs, control of antigravity responses, allowance of erect posture and walking, fine-motor skill development, maintaining proper axial tone and alertness, and inhibiting primitive reflexes. Normal maturation, therefore, involves the process in which the upper system inhibits the lower motor control system; "automatic" is replaced with "voluntary." Persistence of lower system-mediated behaviors is indicative of abnormal function. This approach is reflected in some of the early neurodevelopmental gross motor items in the Bayley-4.

Environment is considered to have minimal impact on maturational approaches to development; however, experience-independent networks and canalized behaviors are compatible with the core concepts of the maturational model. Of note is that maturational theory historically has been highly influential in developmental assessment (including identification of the cephalocaudal and proximodistal courses of development) and has provided the basis for traditional reliance on milestones and age norms in early evaluation of motor function. This approach is reflected in the neuromotor items of the Bayley-4, including inhibition of early reflexes.

Serial assessment

Currently, the permanency of epigenetic changes and modifications is not known; some may be long-term, while others are transient. These issues underscore the need for serial assessment to capture the constantly evolving picture of a child's development and to better account for the contributions of plasticity and epigenetics. In addition to one-time assessments falling short in providing an accurate picture of a child's development, inaccuracy is compounded by rating a developmental skill or acquisition as simply present or absent. Granted the sequence of development is invariant, but because the rate can vary by individual, considering skills as possibly *emerging* versus simply mastered or not present better accounts for the variability that is dependent on underlying brain changes.

Disruption and insult

The discussion thus far has involved infants who have not experienced atypical brain development or damage. However, there are many infants, both full- and preterm, whose early pre-, peri-, or postnatal history includes disruption and/or insult—these "at-risk" individuals comprise a large proportion of children who typically are administered developmental assessments such as the Bayley-4. There exists a "two-hit hypothesis" of negative effects on the infant's brain, particularly in those born prematurely (Aylward, 2018): (1) *developmental disruption*, and (2) *insult*. These two "hits" are not mutually exclusive and the two spheres that represent disruption and insult overlap in some children, suggesting that a number of infants and toddlers will experience both events to varying degrees.

Developmental disruption

Being born prematurely causes disruption of developmentally regulated processes such as the capacity to synthesize protective growth factors, neuronal migration/organization, oligogenesis (development of cells that are involved in myelin production), axonal/neuronal formation, and subsequent myelination (Gilles, Gressens, Dammann, & Leviton, 2017). Essentially, the temporal and spatial trajectories of brain development and architecture are altered.

This raises two issues: (1) neurologic function provides insight into more complex neural networks very early in development, often before these neural networks are conscripted into functional service. Hence, there is a need to evaluate the evolving *neurologic*→*motor*→*sensorimotor*→*cognitive* sequence of increasingly complex developmental functions (Aylward, 2009); and (2) being born early disrupts functional neural networks in parts of the brain that may not be recruited until the child is older. The later appearance of dysfunction is essentially due to a "silent period" where the atypically developed area is not yet called into service. The more complex the network (e.g., involving the projection of long axons), the greater the probability of disruption.

Insult

Actual insult to the brain could be caused by any of the following: inflammation, chorioamnionitis, maternal infection, or hypoxic ischemic encephalopathy (HIE). These processes can result in: (a) subsequent release of glutamate and resultant cell excitotoxicity; (b) a necrosis-apoptosis continuum of cell damage; and (c) insult due to reperfusion and free radicals. Other potential sequelae include altered cortico-thalamic connectivity issues (due to damage to the temporary subplate neuronal layer (existent from 22 to 34 weeks gestation) that acts as a switchboard for ascending and descending neural connections), resultant glial scars, neuronal/axonal damage, white and gray matter microscopic damage, and sequelae of conditions such as periventricular leukomalacia (Douglas-Escobar & Weiss, 2015; Volpe, 2009). In addition to immediate (primary) and slightly delayed (secondary) phases of damage, there is a tertiary phase that occurs months after the insult that will also have an impact on remodeling (Douglas-Escobar & Weiss, 2015).

Developmental disruption is typical in the preterm infant, while insult affects infants regardless of gestational age, although gestational age will determine what areas of the brain are most affected. That is because the areas that have the greatest rates of metabolism are also the most vulnerable. In the term infant, there typically is a sentinel event (e.g., placental insufficiency) that produces hypoxia/ischemia before or during the birth process.

In the preterm infant, immaturity increases vulnerability, and there are both early and late morbidities. After a sentinel event such as hypoxia/ischemia or intraventricular hemorrhage, there are also delayed onset morbidities that include late-onset sepsis, necrotizing enterocolitis (NEC), apnea/bradycardia, anemia, or bronchopulmonary dysplasia (BPD; lung scarring and damage requiring extended supplemental oxygen) which cause further, low-grade but chronic hypoxia (Laptook, 2016). In fact, a recent metaanalysis indicated that BPD is a key factor that affects outcome negatively, above and beyond being born extremely/very preterm (Twilhaar et al., 2018).

The degree and duration of oxygen deprivation, coupled with the gestational age of the infant, will produce different areas of damage and patterns of reorganization in the brain. Often, there is direct brain injury to white matter in terms of lesions or alterations in the microstructure; however, there are secondary gray matter neuronal abnormalities as well (Volpe, 2009). As mentioned earlier, differentiation and segregation of functional circuits shift from short-range circuits (i.e., those in close proximity) to longer-range assemblies that connect to hubs that integrate information—these are very susceptible to injury (Menon, 2013).

Therefore, disruption and insult will add more complexity to the already complicated processes of plasticity and epigenetics and can involve atrophy of brain structures (e.g., prefrontal cortex) and the dopaminergic neurotransmitter system. Brain remodeling via reorganization and recovery will also vary; all reorganization is not necessarily beneficial and can be dysfunctional, leading to "maladaptive plasticity" (Fiori & Guzzetta, 2015). Moreover, if a section of the brain takes over the function of a previously dedicated area (e.g., as in the case of the right hemisphere assuming language functions due to damage to the left hemisphere in a young child), the compensating brain area will lose some of its predetermined capabilities (e.g., in this case, visual-spatial abilities). This is referred to as the "crowding effect" (Fiori & Guzzetta, 2015).

Translating to developmental assessment

The potential for additional insult to occur in the preterm infant's brain after an initial sentinel event results in difficulty estimating the extent of developmental problems early on because of the persistent, contemporary effects of the illness.

Even with the more static damage profile found in full-term infants who were exposed to insult, the potential exists for change in the presentation of the injury. For example, low tone in the first months of life may evolve into spasticity over time. Although simple canalized behaviors tend to be self-righting, other prewired circuits (experience-expectant and experience-dependent) feasibly may suffer unprogrammed cell death via necrosis and apoptosis. Experience-expectant and experience-dependent circuits may have been eliminated or compromised due to cell death, leaving in place maladaptive circuits that normally should have been eliminated via programmed apoptosis.

The need for serial developmental assessment again is evident. The presence of emerging skills (e.g., scores of 1 on the Bayley-4) could be encouraging, being suggestive that at least some of the circuits underlying these skills are intact. Serial assessment will clarify if the child transitions from emerging status to mastery of developmental acquisitions.

We are faced with the challenge to develop techniques that assess the basic, early components of higher-order functions prior to the appearance of more complex behaviors that evolve with increasing age. Functional imaging has shown that certain motor areas of the young child's brain are also activated when he or she is engaged in cognitive activities; similarly, brain areas traditionally associated with cognitive functions come on line when the child is involved in motor tasks (Diamond, 2000). More specifically, the cerebellum and the prefrontal cortex are components of a neural circuit and there are interconnections between both components in a "cross-talk" type of arrangement. These two brain centers work together particularly if: (a) the cognitive task is difficult; (b) the task is novel, versus familiar; (c) a rapid response is needed; or (d) concentration rather than automatic responding is required (Diamond, 2000). The caudate nucleus (part of the striatum, which, in turn, is a component of the limbic system) is also involved as a major output structure of the dorsal lateral prefrontal cortex.

It logically follows that the cerebellum/frontal cortex/striatum circuit would come into play in unison when higher-order executive functions are involved (Van Houdt, Oosterlaan, Van Wassnaer-Leemhuis, Van Kaam, & Aarmpidse-Moens, 2019). These executive functions are interrelated in toddlers and young children and include verbal working memory, visual working memory, processing speed, attention, inhibition, and cognitive flexibility (switching) (Mulder, Hoofs, Verhagen, van der Veen, & Leseman, 2014). However, it is difficult to truly evaluate these more complex behaviors in children below the age of 4 without overtaxing the child's cognitive, attention, language, and motor capabilities. The challenge in relating early developmental assessment to underlying brain development and function is how to initially identify simple, lower-order indicators of these complex skills—the premise being if tasks mediated by these precursor circuits cannot be accomplished, the likelihood of successfully addressing more complex tasks that use these circuits as well as more intricate white matter long-range assemblies (i.e., for executive functions) is markedly reduced. For predictive purposes, early indicators of potential problems in these long-distance circuits need to be identified, acknowledging they will differ in phenotypic presentation (e.g., as in the case of presentation of executive function during infancy and toddlerhood). That is why the Bayley-4 includes tasks that involve attention, novel learning, response speed, and verbal and visual working memory evolving from simple to complex tasks.

Summary of main points

In summary, development involves the acquisition of new capabilities over time which are the result of biological/physical maturation, experiential learning, and emotional, social, and cultural environmental factors. The neuro-environmental synthesis model acknowledges the array of factors that affect brain development and underscores how the environment plays a critical role in this process. This perspective provides the theoretic rationale for selection and scoring of many Bayley-4 items.

Summary of plasticity

The model contains several key premises. First is the concept of *plasticity* defined as the cumulative, dynamic shaping of the brain by both risk and protective factors (Willett, 2018). Some innate cell assemblies are not dependent on external input, but strengthen their interconnections via synchronized firing. Those cell assemblies that are out of synchrony will be pruned. Other circuits are preexisting, but require environmental input for priming; without this environmental input, they too will be eliminated. Still, others are heavily dependent on external input for their development and are critical for formation of integrated neural networks and subsequent learning. Essentially, early on, the CNS responds to the environment in a dynamic manner.

There is also evidence that higher-order, complex cognitive skills involve longer, more geographically distant connections between neurons across white matter pathways. These circuits develop later and are more susceptible to disruption or injury. Because they become functional later, developmental problems that involve these connections may not be evident until later childhood or beyond, and therefore, may not be detected with our current approach to infant testing. This suggests that testing the function of one developmental domain may provide insight as to the integrity of another as well (as in the case of motor and cognitive tasks activating the same brain areas). Plasticity in infants and young children affords more flexibility than in adults because the circuitry is incomplete and dynamic.

Summary of epigenetics

The second premise involves *epigenetics* where genes respond to the environment, with methylation (turning off the activity of certain genes) determining the expression of the DNA without altering the DNA sequence. Methylation is an important component in brain development and neurotransmission.

Disruption/insult summary

Third is the influence of *disruption, insult, or a combination of the two* and how the child's brain will reorganize and recover in response to these events. Because of a history of prematurity or biological insult to the brain, these children are more likely to require developmental evaluation with the Bayley-4. Reorganization is not always beneficial and at times can be maladaptive.

Role of the environment

The *role of the environment* on brain development is important. Environmental influences do not need to be extreme to affect brain growth and organization. Physical exposures, experiences, sensory inputs, and social transactions will differentially affect both plasticity and epigenetics. Deficiencies in brain development caused by the environment vary, based on the neural circuits that are developing at the time of exposure (these are most vulnerable) and the severity of the negative environmental influence. "Toxic stress" is cumulative and takes its toll on the infant's stress response system, particularly the hypothalamic-pituitary-adrenal (HPA) axis. This is assumed to affect development of the prefrontal cortex, amygdala, hippocampus, and also to decrease the number of synapses and impair the process of neurogenesis (Lipina & Posner, 2012). Chronicity and timing effects of the environment on brain structure need further study.

Relationship to assessment

The aim of developmental assessment is to enhance sensitivity (detection of "true positives" with few "false negatives"), while at the same time, maintain good specificity (minimize "false positives"). However, separate, discrete functions may be more highly correlated at a given age than would the same underlying function assessed longitudinally. This is due to qualitative change in the specific function over time which may appear to reflect dyssynchrony. Moreover, if we do not know what the early indicators of these networks are, we cannot test them. Hence, identification of behavioral precursors of these networks needs further investigation so that they can be included in developmental tests.

In terms of development, not only are there changes *within* each neural network, but also changes in the interactions *between* networks. It becomes evident why prediction, particularly in children with low average or borderline functioning, is so difficult.

Some children may be more susceptible or vulnerable to adverse influences than others due to genetic, physiologic, or behavioral attributes. Conversely, these same individual characteristics could cause children to function particularly well under more positive circumstances. These individual differences in plasticity and malleability are termed "differential susceptibility" (Belsky, 2016) to either positive or negative influences, and this will shape the course of the child's development. Both types of differences, viewed in a "for better or for worse" manner (Belsky, 2016), need to be considered in developmental assessment.

In closing, developmental hypotheses continually are negated and replaced by new hypotheses that do a better job of explaining empirical findings (Paneth, 2018). The ontogeny of increasingly complex brain function will provide these new insights. Therefore, this neuro-environmental synthesis model will continue to evolve as our understanding of brain development and environment expands and is refined. Longitudinal versus cross-sectional studies are necessary to determine how changes in the brain parallel changes in behavior assessed with developmental tests (Guyer et al., 2018). Hopefully, this increased understanding and refinement will also lead to advances in developmental assessment, the Bayley-4 being the most current step in that direction. Stay tuned.

CHAPTER 2
The new test

Contents

Reasons for a revision

Developmental assessment incorporates three interrelated elements:

- administration of structured test items (e.g., acquired skills, learning, problem solving);
- direct observation of typical and atypical behaviors and milestones;
- active participation of the parent or caregiver in the evaluation process, including collecting information provided by the caregiver and caregiver report.

In addition to these three elements, historical information assists in interpretation of results. Using these components as a framework, various changes in the Bayley were implemented. Experiential bias with regard to structured test items was limited to better reflect true learning ability and capacity to adjust to new situational demands, versus what the child has or has not been exposed to. Experiential bias involves the child having had experience with tasks such as stacking blocks, placing pegs, cutting with scissors, or completing form boards; advanced performance could be due to familiarity with similar manipulatives at home (blocks, pegboards, scissors) or teaching to task in early intervention programs.

A balance between assessing the broad range of developmental skills and simultaneously keeping the overall administration time within a reasonable duration to minimize fatigue and refusals is necessary. Achieving

Bayley 4 Clinical Use and Interpretation
https://doi.org/10.1016/B978-0-12-817754-9.00002-7

this balance produces more accurate and valid data and maintains both the child's and examiner's sanity.

Although a larger item pool enhances reliability and samples more aspects of the broad concept of development, if a test is too lengthy because of an all-inclusive mindset, the validity of the data regarding infant's ability will be compromised.

The Bayley-4 was designed to address these two issues in several ways. First, in many cases behaviors can be scored by incidental observation while the child engages in testing. These items are found in the Test Behavior Checklist. Caregivers are participants in the assessment and structured caregiver questions are meant to ascertain that the behavior under review is "typical," decrease anxiety in the caregiver and the child due to examiner effects, and therefore, improve the quality of the evaluation. Caregiver report also better describes the child's abilities across settings, versus the "snapshot" taken in a 60-minute (on a good day) clinic session. Missing scores due to refusals are minimized. This approach also addresses some of the issues raised by "authentic assessment" advocates (e.g., Bagnato, Neisworth, & Pretti-Frontczak, 2010) and procedures and process criticisms are reduced to a significant degree.

At the outset, the Bayley-4 revision was geared to address several major goals that are outlined below.

Maintain the basic qualities of the Bayley scales

The theoretical rationale of the scales and test items within them generally remain eclectic, although the neuro-environmental synthesis orientation (as outlined in Chapter 1) has influenced the Bayley-4 approach to developmental assessment. Test items assess the major developmental domains and these are administered in the standardized, norm-referenced testing model.

The five-scale framework of the Bayley-III is maintained in the fourth edition. A balance was struck to improve scoring (and add, combine, or delete items), yet still preserve comparability to the Bayley-III. Historically, it was difficult to switch from a two-scale Mental Developmental Index (MDI) and Psychomotor Developmental Index (PDI) model found on the original Bayley and Bayley-II, to the Cognitive, Language (expressive and receptive communication), Motor (fine and gross), Adaptive, and Social-Emotional Scales of the Bayley-III. Various attempts to reconcile the scoring differences between the two formats were attempted, but generally these were not successful (see Aylward, 2013; Aylward & Aylward, 2011). Moreover, the MDI and PDI dichotomy each contained items that arguably could be included on either scale. Therefore, rather than initiating another round of attempts at reconciliation and consternation if the Bayley-4 were changed significantly, it was decided to maintain the same format. Although criticized for a variety of other reasons, the Bayley-III framework is particularly useful for early intervention purposes and longitudinal studies. However, it is not economical time-wise to test the same function several times with related, highly correlated items. Redundancy was, therefore, reduced by eliminating similar items. This approach did not have a negative effect on scores, as comparison of the Bayley-III and Bayley-4, administered to 184 children in a counter-balanced fashion, revealed a mean 1-point difference (Cognitive Composite 1 point, Language 0.5 points, and Motor 1.3 points) (see Aylward & Zhu, 2019).

Develop a polytomous scoring approach

Development is on a continuum that is dynamic and uneven; therefore, a dichotomous scoring approach (i.e., 1, 0) used on previous versions of the Bayley was not considered adequate to capture a child's true developmental status at any given point in time. More specifically, there is a clear distinction between an infant who displays mastery of a developmental skill from one who absolutely does not. However, many children show emerging abilities that are not at the mastery level, but are present to some degree. These children differ from infants who have achieved mastery, but they also differ from those who do not display the skill at all. With a dichotomous scoring approach, children who show some evidence of the skill would not be distinguished from those in whom the skill was totally absent (i.e., both would be given a 0 score). This has an impact on the contemporary accuracy of scores and prediction and does not differentiate a temporary delay from a possible long-term deficit. Therefore, a polytomous scoring approach (i.e., 2, 1, 0) was developed for the Bayley-4. The clinician is encouraged to conceptualize the polytomous scoring framework as:

- **2 points**: This score reflects successful mastery of a task or skill. A 2-point score reflects proficiency that occurs consistently or *almost all of the time* (≥75%). This would apply to caregiver report as well.
- **1 point**: The 1-point scoring option is used in the case of an emerging skill or performance that does not indicate mastery on a task, but the skill is present to some degree. The skill may be inconsistent, an approximation of the desired response, or *present some of the time* (i.e., <75%). Essentially, it is partially acquired and is anticipated to eventually evolve into mastery. This framework is also appropriate for caregiver report.

- **0 points:** This score is given when the skill is *absent or not present*; it is not clear as to whether the absence of the skill reflects a delay or a deficit. Caregiver report again would use the same guidelines.
  The examiner should not pursue a "2" response if the infant demonstrated clear-cut behavior that met the criteria for a "1." This would be a potential issue only for a very limited number of items because scoring criteria for time, items pointed to or named, number of blocks stacked, etc. are rigorously defined.

To illustrate application of this scoring format, consider the developmental progression found in the gross motor item, "*Jumps: both feet*" (GM 48). A 2-point response (mastery) is achieved if the child jumps with both feet being off the floor at the same time, or if the child leads with one foot but both feet are in the air at some point during the jump. A 1-point response is assigned if the child jumps with one foot in the air, while the other still provides support on the ground, does not show good balance, or the child can do the task only some of the time. This reflects the emergence of the capacity to jump off the floor with both feet. The 0-point scoring option is selected if the child bends his or her legs in an attempt to jump but both feet remain in contact (as if "glued") with the floor or simply does not show any effort or approximation of a jump. This level of performance does not suggest the emergence of the skill necessary to jump.

Similarly, the "*reaches for/touches block*" item (FM 12) demonstrates the concept of complete acquisition of a skill (mastery) as well as a developmental progression. A 2-point response involves the child successfully extending his or her arm and touching the block in a consistent manner; 1 point (emerging) is given if the child attempts to reach for the block, but typically is not successful or can do so only some of the time—the beginning of fine motor coordination and planning is evident. The 0-point score option is used if the child does not attempt to reach for the block, indicating that this skill is not at the emergent stage.

Mastery, as evident by how the child approaches a task, is illustrated by the "*plays with paper*" item (C 18) which measures inquisitiveness and exploratory behavior. The infant receives 2 points by scratching, crinkling, or mouthing the paper, and being interested in the sound and/or texture; a 1-point response reflects a brief interest where the infant may reach for the paper but does not manipulate it—approach, exploration, and interest are fleeting. With the 0-point response, the infant may look at the paper but not attempt to touch it, indicating a lack of interest or approach.

The motor item, "*foot grasp (Plantar)*" *(GM 19)*, is a bit different in conceptualization. It is neuromaturational and is an example of cortical function inhibiting a lower brain-center-mediated reflex (Amiel-Tison & Gosselin, 2008). Two points are given if *no* spontaneous plantar grasp is observed when the examiner's thumbs are pressed against the bottom of the child's foot, suggesting that the reflex is now inhibited by higher brain function; 1 point is assigned when the elicited foot grasp is transient, but still occasionally present, indicating that inhibition is progressing but not complete; 0 points would be assigned if the infant maintains a strong, consistent foot grasp, underscoring a lack of cortical inhibition and possible underlying dysfunction.

Frequency and consistency of the desired response are assessed in the "*Says 3 -word sentences*" item (EC 25). Two points are given when the child *consistently* produces three-word sentences or longer strings of words; 1 point is assigned when the child *occasionally (< 75% of the time)* produces a three-word sentence, indicating low frequency or inconsistent behavior; the 0-point option is given for sentences less than three words or for *not producing* word combinations at all.

Timed items such as the pegboard (e.g., C 38, 46) or form board series (C 43, 49, 55) categorize mastery in terms of processing speed, defined by the number of pieces placed or the time taken to complete the task.

Finally, the sequence of development is invariant, but the rate of progression through the sequence varies; the three-option scoring system helps to differentiate infants and toddlers who display a slower developmental rate (emerging) from those who receive numerous scores of 0. Children in the latter group may be displaying early developmental trajectories that are indicative of a deficit. With a dichotomous scoring system, both of these trajectories would be grouped together and contrasted to infants with "average" developmental slopes, thereby causing the clinician to miss important diagnostic data.

Include caregivers in the evaluation process

The use of caregiver report should not be the sole source of information in developmental assessment, but information provided by the caregiver is very helpful in obtaining a better understanding of the child's abilities, reducing testing time, and minimizing missing scores. Caregiver report is now routinely used in developmental screening (American Academy of Pediatrics, 2006) and has also been successfully applied to children at medical/biological risk (Aylward & Verhulst, 2008; Blaggan et al., 2014;

Johnson, Wolke, & Marlow, 2008; Martin et al., 2013). Whereas prior to the last 10–15 years, screening tests that rely on parent report were considered Level I (preliminary) assessments, parent report has evolved to a higher, Level II status, with screening now being based solely on parent report. This is exemplified by use of the PEDS (Glascoe, 1998) and the Ages and Stages-3 (Bricker & Squires, 2009).

Caregiver report was utilized in administration of the Bayley Infant Neurodevelopmental Screener (BINS; Aylward, 1995) and served as an impetus to include formal caregiver responses for the Bayley-4. With respect to the BINS, parent report was necessary because the number of items in each age range was limited (11–13), causing missing data due to refusals or ambiguous responses to be problematic. The utility of parent report was also evaluated by having parents view a video that depicted infants engaged in BINS items, scoring how the caregiver thought his or her child would perform on the item, and then having the BINS administered by examiners blinded to the caregiver's scoring. Overall agreement ranged from 70% to 83%. On the BINS standard administration, a maximum of two caregiver-reported responses were permitted (Aylward & Verhulst, 2008).

A total of 57 Bayley-4 items can be scored using caregiver responses. Selection of these items was based on a literature review, examiner experience, and characteristics of the individual items. Most parent report items are found on the Expressive Communication scale (24), followed by Receptive Communication and Gross Motor (6 and 11, respectively). The Cognitive and Fine Motor scales have the fewest parent report items (9 and 7, respectively).

The Bayley-4 items that utilize the caregiver question format were selected based on literature that indicated expressive language-related items and items that assess motor development have a higher likelihood of refusal in infants and toddlers (Aylward, 2009; Skellern, Rogers, & O'Callaghan, 2001). Children are more likely to refuse items that are difficult for them, and self-awareness of such difficulty emerges early in development. These refusals make it more difficult to determine if the child does or does not possess a skill and cause scores be more difficult to interpret. Caregiver report also allows for verification of behavior that was ambiguous or not observed during testing. For example, items involving representational (C 50) or imaginary play (C 59) tap higher order cognitive abilities, but they are difficult to administer in routine Bayley clinical assessments because they require spontaneity and a major switch in the testing format. Although these behaviors are good indicators of complex cognitive processes, they are often time-consuming to administer, difficult to elicit, frequently refused, and have a greater likelihood of occurring in familiar, versus clinic, surroundings. As a result, these items are now scored *exclusively* by parent report.

Use of caregiver report also allows for a more "naturalistic" or "authentic" assessment (Macy, Bagnato, Macy, & Salaway, 2015). Caregiver responses are used to obtain additional information for those behaviors that are more easily observed on a day-to-day basis in a naturalistic setting such as the home (e.g., visually inspects hands, intelligibility of verbalizations, banging objects, or social routines). Vocalizations and verbal behaviors are often limited in assessment situations due to shyness or refusals. In response, a variety of receptive and expressive communication items, particularly the latter, were also selected for the caregiver question format option.

Caregiver questions are not utilized for items that involve performance on test-specific tasks such as form boards, pegboards, or stacking blocks, because caregivers most likely have not observed the child engage in these activities and these tasks must be administered using standardized procedures and materials. While there is the potential for caregiver bias, questions are posed in a specific manner with allowance for inquiry when the response is vague. A specific structure is provided to the caregiver at the outset in order to standardize report, namely: (a) *almost all the time*: the child is able to perform the task at least 75% or ¾ of the time; (b) *some of the time*: the child is able to perform a task at least one time or occasionally, but not 75% of the time; or (c) *does not display the behavior* at all. The wording of the caregiver questions is standardized and specific. In addition to the *every/some/none* question indicated above, there is also *an often, not often, or not at all* option (e.g., C 19, bangs object), or questions where the caregiver is requested to provide examples (e.g., imaginary or representational play items; C 50, 59). Caregiver responses should not be employed for the sole purpose of increasing the child's score.

To summarize, it is recommended items that include caregiver report be used judiciously and in the following scenarios: (1) When certain responses, particularly those on observational items, are ambiguous in their interpretation; (2) When the child's rate of refusals jeopardizes the validity of test findings; and (3) on certain play items on the cognitive scale (e.g., representational, imaginary) that are scored solely by caregiver report. Of note is the fact that, during standardization, all appropriate-for-age caregiver reports (administered in a standardized format) were scored, as were observational and administered items. The caregiver mean scores (cognitive, language, and motor) and those from actually observed or administered items differed by

0.01 to 0.04 points (overall mean difference = 0.02 which was not significant), indicating that the scores could be used interchangeably. Therefore, caregiver report was also represented in the normative data.

Reduction of testing duration time/simplifying administration

The balance between the conceptual and the pragmatic (or practical) approaches with regard to the length of a test was an issue with previous versions of the Bayley. It was estimated that the average time for a 13-month-old infant to compete the Bayley-III was 90 minutes. To my knowledge, there are very few 13-month-olds who would remain engaged for that amount of time. Infants and toddlers have a limited attention span, fatigue easily, have no investment in what their scores will be, and are more prone to test refusals. Therefore, one of the prime goals of the Bayley-4 was to strike a balance between having a robust, representative item set, while simultaneously reducing administration time. This was addressed by combining items, eliminating redundant items that measure the same constructs (i.e., highly correlated; $r > 0.79$), and reducing the upper limit of time allotted for completion of various test tasks. Caregiver report and the Bayley-4 digital capture program (Q-Global) also helped tremendously in that regard.

The child's age and level of function (i.e., exceptional, average, delayed) will have an impact on the length of the testing session. Children with greater impairment may require additional time to complete tasks or understand the task demands; conversely, the total number of items administered most likely would be reduced, possibly truncating administration time. Children functioning in the exceptional or highly exceptional range will have a higher ceiling and take more time before the required discontinue criterion of five consecutive scores of 0 is obtained. The reason for testing also is a major consideration; if the purpose is to rule out delay, the need for high-end testing becomes moot. This is also the rationale behind not expanding the number of advanced items—in fact, they were reduced somewhat.

During standardization, all caregiver questions were presented as were all trials of any given item even if discontinued criteria were met. In addition, many examiners were unfamiliar with Bayley-4 items and there was an extended ceiling before discontinuation. These factors would serve to increase administration time. Nonetheless, 50th percentile times were recorded for the following age groups for the entire Bayley-4 using the Q-Global format (see Chapter 12); (Bayley & Aylward, 2019a, 2019b):

• 16 days to 6 months, 30 days	34 minutes
• 7 months to 12 months, 30 days	41 minutes
• 13 months to 18 months, 30 days	58 minutes
• 19 months to 24 months, 30 days	66 minutes
• 25 months to 30 months, 30 days	66 minutes
• 31 to 36 months	68 minutes
• 37 to 42 months	69 minutes

Improve age and content coverage

Based on the neuro-environmental synthesis model, special effort was made to include items that assess neurodevelopmental function and early forms of executive functioning (EF). Neurodevelopmental items provide early indications of possible central nervous system dysfunction (Amiel-Tison & Gosselin, 2008; Milani-Comparetti & Gidoni, 1967) and reflect the fact that our ability to assess infants evolves from the neurologic → motor → sensorimotor → cognitive function (Aylward, 2009).

Development proceeds from a *basic skill* (e.g., reaching, grasping) to a *function* (reaching, grasping, and bringing an object to the mouth), to an *integrated functional unit* (overcoming a barrier to obtain an object that is then brought to the mouth). The functional unit involves integration and coordination of various discrete functions such as problem solving, planning, and object permanency, forming the basis for later intelligence (Aylward, 2009). This involves integration of different neural networks (see Chapter 1). Our earliest window to this developmental sequence is found in early neurodevelopmental and executive functioning indicators. There is also evidence that early neurodevelopmental problems place a child at greater risk for later cognitive and motor difficulties (Amiel-Tison & Gosselin, 2008).

In regard to executive functions, these change over the course of infancy through adolescence. In infancy, self-regulation involves arousal. This initially is extrinsically controlled (via input from the caregiver) and subsequently evolves to intrinsic regulation (Taylor & Clark, 2016). Over time, EF moves from a general factor to distinct component functions (Wiebe, Espy, & Charak, 2008). Executive function becomes more sophisticated with age, as the toddler must mentally represent the goal to be achieved, filter out competing stimuli, plan, and adjust to environmental contingencies. This capacity is sometimes referred to as "cognitive control" (Diamond, 2013). Use of working memory, inhibitory control, and cognitive flexibility increases markedly from age 2 to 5 (Diamond, 2013; see Chapter 1).

Nonetheless, there is continued disagreement as to whether executive function can be conceptualized as distinct component skills or a unified core function in young children (Garon, Bryson, & Smith, 2006; Wiebe et al., 2008). Based on current data, it appears that EF is more of a core, self-regulatory function in infants (Beck, Schaefer, Pang, & Carlson, 2011). "Heterotypic continuity" exists where patterns of self-regulation are manifest in different ways during development (Taylor & Clark, 2016). For example, executive function is first evident when an infant becomes aware and selectively attends to the environment (Rothbart & Posner, 2001). EF is also reflected in habituation (Rueda, Posner, & Rothbart, 2005; Turk-Brown, Scholl, & Chun, 2008). Both of these indicators are included in the Bayley-4 (CG 3, 4, 8, 10). With increasing age, executive functions become more specialized and evolve from reactive to proactive (Beck et al., 2011). EF tasks often used with preschoolers include the "A-not-B task" (Diamond, 1990, 2013), "standard dimensional change card sort," and the "Go/no-go task" (Espy et al., 2002; Wiebe et al., 2011). These tasks were not included in the Bayley-4 because they would significantly increase test administration time and be restricted to higher ages (Carlson, 2005).

Increase sensitivity

A criticism of the Bayley-III, in addition to its length, involved suspected inflation of test norms (Anderson, De Luca, Hutchinson, Roberts, & Doyle, 2010; Aylward, 2013; Aylward & Aylward, 2011). This was considered to be due in part to inclusion of approximately 10% of "at-risk" infants and toddlers in the normative sample. The premise for seeding these infants and toddlers in the normative sample was that this reflects the diversity found in the normal population (Aylward, 2013; Pena, Spaulding, & Plante, 2006). The procedure would also add additional variance, thereby enhancing correlations. It is not clear if these at-risk infants and toddlers were distributed evenly across all age ranges of the normative sample or if the degree of risk was comparable. However, in a recent white paper (Aylward & Zhu, 2019) comparison of scores including and scores excluding the at-risk infants and toddlers revealed less than a 1-point difference (Cognitive scaled score difference = 0.16; Language Composite score difference = 0.61; and Motor Composite = 0.98), indicating this was not as big of an issue as once thought.

Furthermore, the Bayley-II scores were lower than the original Bayley (MDI by 12 points; PDI by 7 points). In contrast, the Bayley-III scores were *higher* than those of the Bayley-II (Cognitive 6–10 points; Motor 8–18 points).

While it is possible that the Bayley-II underestimates development (Hack et al., 2005), this does not explain the mean cognitive scores of 108 in an extremely preterm Australian sample or 118 in matched controls (Anderson et al., 2010). These findings may also reflect the fact that the MDI is not directly comparable to the Cognitive Composite or the PDI differs from the Motor Composite. Also, the Bayley-II had restricted item sets and different basal and ceiling rules, thereby truncating scores (Aylward & Zhu, 2019).

It was hypothesized that minimizing the inclusion of "at-risk" children in the normative sample and use of the polytomous scoring approach would enhance sensitivity. Specificity on the Bayley-III may have been high because there were few false positives. In fact, many investigators have moved the previous cut-off score for developmental disability from 2 SDs below average (70) to 1 SD (85) or 1.3 SD (~80) below the mean score of 100 (Vohr et al., 2012). It is not clear, however, if this approach would be equally applicable to cognitive, language, and motor function.

Improve the clinical utility of the Bayley

To evaluate the clinical utility of the Bayley-4, special group studies were conducted during the scale's tryout and standardization phases. Data were collected on 412 infants and toddlers with established and biological risk conditions which place them at developmental jeopardy. These groups include: (1) extremely (EPT; <28 weeks gestation) and very preterm infants (VPT; <32 weeks); (2) moderate and late preterm infants (MPT/LPT; 32–33 and 34–36 weeks); (3) children with Autism Spectrum Disorder; (4) infants and toddlers with Down syndrome; (5) children having language delay/impairment; (6) infants displaying motor impairment (CP and DCD); (7) children prenatally exposed to drugs/alcohol; and (8) those with identified developmental delay. The special group studies provide initial clinical validity evidence (discriminant and diagnostic) for the Bayley-4 and special group studies are described in Chapter 11. Suffice it to say that the clinical groups differed from matched controls in all comparisons.

The main purpose of the Bayley-4 is to detect developmental delays. In designing the test, I was not as interested in how advanced a child might be so that they could qualify for preschool Ivy League feeder programs or the parents could compare DQs on playdates. Concerns were expressed by some examiners that Bayley-III basal items might be too easy at certain ages and credit was given for previous items that, had they been administered, would not be successfully completed. In response, more easy items and partial credit (score of 1) were included to refine assessment at the low end. A goal was to monitor item gradients so that small changes in raw scores would not produce major changes in scaled scores (this would have an impact on age equivalents as well). Items measuring acquired skills, learning, and problem solving were specifically included to improve clinical utility.

Use digital administration

The Bayley-4 Q-Global (B4QG) digital capture (see Chapter 12) was developed to facilitate test administration by recording responses, scoring items, simultaneously scoring more advanced but related items (e.g., blocks, form boards, pegboard), as well as automatically calculating basal and ceiling values. The digital capture format also allows flexibility in administration (i.e., it is nonlinear). The B4QG was designed to reduce testing time and transform the user experience to a state-of-the-art level. The digital capture is designed to support administration that maximizes efficiency, reduces the need to have a separate manual open during testing, and prevents administration errors. The Bayley-4 Q-Global is designed for use on tablets, laptops, and PCs. The digital capture acts as a "superego" of sorts, by ensuring proper start points, that basal and ceiling rules are followed, and computation of the child's age and scores is accurate.

Finally, examiners can more easily switch from one item set to another, allowing flexibility. Change in administration order did not affect scores on the Bayley-III; therefore, this was not considered to be an issue with the Bayley-4.

Growth scale values

Growth Scale Values (GSV) can also be used to improve the clinical utility of the Bayley-4, if the examiner elects to use this option. This metric is essentially unchanged from the Bayley-III, but has been de-emphasized due to the lack of widespread use. Basically, GSV enable longitudinal tracking of a child's developmental growth over time by comparing raw scores at different test administrations. This option is available for the five subtests (cognitive, receptive and expressive language, and fine and gross motor) and is based on the total *raw score* of the individual subtest. GSV are objective scores with an absolute, equal-interval scale. The mean is 500, and the SD is 100. The child's performance is measured independent of peers and the GSV is sensitive to small amounts of change that might not be apparent when scaled scores are compared to peers. The GSV is more sensitive to small developmental gains than are scaled scores.

The time interval between two testing sessions is not specified. Therefore, in the case where there is no growth between two assessments, the absence of change may be due to an insufficient time period between the two sessions, a normal developmental plateau, or actual deficits. Conversely, an increase in GSV may be indicative of growth in developmental skills which was not existent previously, or this raw score increase may be influenced by interventions that teach to task, familiarity with the testing situation, or the child being more cooperative. When a decrease in scores occurs, testing issues, neurodevelopmental or environmental factors, and the negative effects of a recent trauma or illness such as bacterial meningitis should be considered. Actual GSV growth charts for the five subtests that were available on the Bayley-III, but are not included in the Bayley-4.

Why adopt a new test?

There have been several articles suggesting caution regarding decisions about adopting new versions of psychological and neuropsychological tests (e.g., Bush et al., 2018). This opinion would also apparently extend to the Bayley-4. The major premise of this conservative approach is that the publication of a newer version of a test does not automatically render a previous version obsolete, nor should adoption occur just because the test is new. Specified conditions supporting adoption of a new test include: (a) new, improved normative data, (b) improved ease of administration, (c) the revision requires less time for administration, (d) it addresses new constructs (such as neurodevelopmental functions, EF, etc.), and (e) there is appropriate inclusion of special clinical populations. The Bayley-4 meets these five conditions and the decision to adopt the test is justified.

CHAPTER 3

The Cognitive scale

Contents

Overview

The Cognitive scale was reduced to 81 items. Bayley-III items were not included in the Bayley-4 Cognitive scale if: (a) they were highly correlated ($r > 0.79$) or redundant; (b) the administration was too complex or time-consuming (e.g., multischeme play); (c) there was a low pass rate; (d) the item was more strongly related to other subscales (e.g., Bayley-III removes lid from bottle, or laces card would be more appropriate in the fine motor subscale); (e) the item was strongly affected by the aforementioned experiential bias (e.g., scissors); or (f) the item introduced a behavior that had the strong likelihood of negatively influencing subsequent items (e.g., taking cubes *out* of cup precedes the item requiring placing cubes *in* the cup). In addition, some items were combined (e.g., response to mirror; various timed items).

New items were added primarily to provide better discrimination at the lower end of function (e.g., an easier puzzle; credit given for a lower number of completed components on several tasks), and others were modified. New artwork was incorporated throughout and many test items and components were altered. For example, the ducks caught the children's interest, but rather than addressing tasks such as grouping, matching by color, size, or patterns, many children would play with "mommy" and "baby" ducks

Bayley 4 Clinical Use and Interpretation
https://doi.org/10.1016/B978-0-12-817754-9.00003-9

according to their own agenda. Though often creative, the children did not receive credit for the items. Other distracting "toys" were deleted as well (e.g., teddy bear). As mentioned earlier, the new, polytomous scoring format and caregiver report were utilized.

The goal of the changes was to improve, economize, and attempt to apply a logical rationale for inclusion of items, yet at the same time not change the scale radically so as to make it difficult to compare to the previous Bayley-III Cognitive scale and frustrate test users.

It would be erroneous to consider the Cognitive scale devoid of a language component (particularly receptive communication) because many of the items incorporate language in the instructions. In fact, the MDI of the Bayley-II was more strongly correlated with the Language scale of the Bayley-III (*r*'s = 0.71–0.87) than with the Cognitive scale (*r*'s = 0.60–0.65) (Aylward, 2013; Bayley, 2006). Therefore, the Cognitive scale can potentially be affected by receptive language impairment. Similarly, it is difficult to separate cognitive skills from fine motor/sensorimotor abilities, particularly at younger ages. Hence, motor problems may have a negative impact as well.

Test items vary in the level of complexity and the hypothesized level of integration of neural networks needed for mastery of the item, due in part to age issues (Armstrong & Agazzi, 2010). The most complex cognitive test items involve information processing which includes thinking, reasoning, short-term verbal and visual memory, and synthesis of information (e.g., Aylward, 1988). Referring back to Chapter 1, it is most likely that highly complex, geographically distant circuits are involved, comprised of experience-dependent synapses; local clusters of information processing circuits are involved as well.

The NIH Toolbox Early Childhood Cognition Battery (for ages 3–6) includes several key cognitive functions that are measured in early childhood (see Brito et al., 2019). These functions are cognitive flexibility (as demonstrated in the card sort task), inhibitory control and attention, processing speed (pattern comparison), episodic memory (pattern sequence memory), and picture vocabulary. Essentially, the battery is heavily loaded with executive function items. There are individual scores as well as an Early Childhood Composite score. Of note, many of these functions are also tapped in the upper age ranges of the Bayley-4. Particularly important is the inclusion of picture vocabulary in the toolbox with the nonverbal tasks so as to round out the assessment of cognition. This suggests the development of a combined Bayley-4 Cognitive and Language Composite score which may be considered in the future to provide an estimate of the child's overall cognitive skills.

Underlying skills that are assessed

Cognitive tasks that incorporate attention, problem solving, learning, concepts (colors (CG 62, 69), classification (CG 69), size (CG 66, 71), weight (CG 65)), detection of patterns (CG 68, 75, 81), short-term/working memory (CG 60, 80), goal directedness, planning, and appreciation of cause-effect relationships are most informative and considered to be indicative of later "intelligence." These higher order tasks also provide a measure of overall brain network efficiency.

Appreciation of numerical concepts (1-to-1 correspondence, counting, cardinality), object permanency, imitation, and imagination in activities such as play also require integration of neural networks. Interestingly, play is thought to promote cognitive growth; however, more complex play skills most likely are also the end *result* of cognitive growth. In addition, habituation, development of visual gestalts/visual perception, and timed items (measuring processing speed and efficiency) are also found in the Cognitive scale and are considered indicative of advanced cognitive abilities. There is debate regarding the utility of timed items in developmental testing; however, timed tests measure the child's speed of information processing, and therefore, are useful.

Many of the underlying skills that have been mentioned undergo changes in their presentation and, therefore, require variation in how they can be assessed over time. Moreover, it is difficult to classify an item given to an infant as being specific to one underlying function. As an overall rule in development, it appears that generality precedes specificity. This is true for developmental testing as well. For example, learning is involved in most tasks on the Cognitive scale. In terms of assessment, learning is first developed in a social context, namely associative learning experienced in caregiver-infant interactions. This type of learning (and memory) includes items that involve response to caregivers, recognition of caregiver, and anticipation of being picked up by an adult (CG 1, 5, 6, 7) and this learning extends to gradations of reaction to the infant's own reflection in a mirror (CG 16). Learning is also involved in habituation (CG 3, 10) and is based on sensory processes (auditory, visual). Faster habituation suggests more efficient learning capabilities, the ability to quickly detect changes in environmental input, and possibly, better inhibitory capacity.

Young children's learning processes can also be assessed by *how* they explore items such as a rattle or even their own hands (CG 15). Imitation involves learning by observation and then applying this newfound skill in similar situations (banging hands on table (CG 20), use of test items such as the spoon and cup (CG 29) or duck and spoon (CG 57)). More advanced learning that is dependent on prior experience includes appreciation of concepts such as colors (CG 62, 69), classification (66), size (63, 71), and weight (CG 65). These items also tap acquired knowledge, and to a lesser extent, concurrent learning that is involved in active problem solving. Early problem solving is demonstrated when the child figures out that a ring can be obtained by pulling on a string (CG 22), uses a pencil to obtain something out of reach (CG 48), removes a pellet from a bottle (CG 34), circumvents an obstacle to obtain an object (CG 35), completes a reversed form board (CG 51), or discerns abstract patterns (CG 68, 75, 79, 81). Performance on these tasks offers insight into the child's capacity and flexibility to *apply* abilities afforded by integrated networks in novel situations. This type of learning is less dependent on experience with specific items.

Working memory is first observed in appreciation of object permanency (CG 7, 21, 37). This increases in complexity from looking for the caregiver or a dropped toy (CG 21), to the examiner removing blocks from a cup without the infant seeing this occur (CG 28) and then to tasks of increasing difficulty such as hiding blocks under cups (CG 32). As the child ages, tasks include anticipation of where the examiner's face will appear from behind a screen, matching pictures after a brief delay, and memory for card placements (CG 56, 76). All involve visual working memory. Auditory short-term memory tasks include memory for words and number sequences (CG 64, 80). Association of names and faces involves both auditory and visual memory skills (CG 60). Essentially, working memory allows the infant and young child to hold information "on line" so that multistep problem solving is possible.

Visual attention (e.g., looking at objects, eye tracking) is involved in a host of cognitive items, as is processing speed. It is acknowledged that the child's motivational state and degree of interest tend to challenge our measurement of processing speed, and as a result, the number of timed items was restricted on the Bayley-4. On most occasions where timing was involved, the maximum duration was decreased to prevent the test from being drawn out and to minimize frustration for the child. As an executive function, attention also enables the infant to sustain performance.

Tasks with the highest levels of cognitive sophistication are those that tap conceptualization and imagination. These involve making believe that an object is something else (e.g., a ball is a piece of fruit, a stick is a sword) or pretending to "use" imaginary objects (e.g., putting imaginary "food" in a plate, walking an imaginary pet) (CG 50, 59). These are critical items in that if the child can successfully demonstrate mastery of these skills, the likelihood of developmental delays or deficits is low (see the discussion of optimality in Chapter 10). The downside is that these items are difficult to administer, in part because they differ in format or involve transitions that may confuse the child. In response, many of these items are now scored solely by caregiver report.

Separation of these early executive functions into discrete components in infants and toddlers is difficult because these functions are more general and intertwined. The EFs separate and become more refined as the child ages. Similarly, it is the *system of connectivity* rather than discrete, individual areas of the brain that are responsible for these behaviors.

To summarize, attention has a major role in learning and the acquisition of information, speed of information processing, and later cognitive development (Cuevas & Bell, 2014). Learning is also related to memory and inhibitory control, the latter perhaps being the most widely studied process in young children. These related functions are considered in the assessment of cognitive abilities on the Bayley-4.

Scoring and interpretation

There are several levels of interpretation that are available, depending on the purpose of the evaluation. Note that steps followed by an asterisk are recommended for *all* administered subtests.

General: Correct for prematurity up to age 2 years at minimum. This is done automatically with the B4QG. For those children born ≥4 months premature, consider cognitive correction to 3 years (Aylward, 2019). Recent data also indicate that it might be helpful to entertain correction of motor and language skills even up to age 3 years (Aylward, 2019).

Level I

- Presentation of standardized score, namely the Cognitive Composite score (M = 100, SD = 15).*
    - The Scaled score (M = 10; SD = 3) is not necessary when describing the cognitive score results by themselves, but is useful when comparing the child's performance in the cognitive domain to subdomains comprising the Language Composite (receptive communication, expressive communication) and the Motor Composite (fine and gross motor).

- Percentile*
- 95% confidence interval*
- Level of function*
    - Extremely High (Very exceptional), > 129;
    - Very High (Exceptional), 120–129;
    - High average, 110–119;
    - Average, 90–109;
    - Low average, 80–89;
    - Very Low (Borderline), 70–79;
    - Extremely low, < 70;
- Age equivalent*
- Percent delay (if applicable)*

Level II

- Discrepancy comparisons (pairwise) at 0.10 or 0.05 levels (preferably the latter so as to be more conservative and to minimize false positives)*
- Standard scores compared within and between subdomains*
- Suggestive cognitive indicators from the ASD checklist (Chapter 8) combined with those from other scales as well*

Level III

- Describe strengths and weaknesses based on item groupings listed earlier in this chapter. For example, sensorimotor items, primarily visual perceptual items, or those involving visual discrimination, though important, are not strongly indicative of complex neural circuitry (which is assumed to underlie later cognitive abilities). Conversely, tasks that incorporate learning, conceptualization, abstracting, working memory, and attention are more complex, most likely reflect activity of underlying, more intricate neural networks, and lend insight as to expectations with regard to later cognitive function. Test items involving conceptualization and imagination are particularly useful in that regard. The ability to perform these subanalyses is dependent on the child's age to a significant degree, although earlier indicators of underlying executive functions and other cognitive processes exist, but will differ in presentation over infancy and toddlerhood (e.g., alertness/attention, habituation, inhibition).
- When appropriate, these findings should be related to historical information, such as established, medical/biological, or environmental risks or protective factors*.
- Relate Cognitive function to the Adaptive and Social Emotional scales if these have also been administered*.

Case example

JJ is seen in the NICU follow-up clinic program for his 2-year visit because he met the gestational age criterion for enrollment. JJ was born at 26 weeks gestational age (extremely preterm; EPT), with a birth weight of 800 g. His neonatal course included Grade III intraventricular hemorrhage (IVH), respiratory distress syndrome (RDS), bronchopulmonary dysplasia (BPD), Grade II retinopathy of prematurity (ROP), apnea and bradycardia, and hyperbilirubinemia. He remained in the hospital for 94 days after birth. JJ's parents are very involved with the toddler, and his mom now stays at home (she was an elementary school teacher); his dad is an executive. JJ receives regular physical and occupational therapy and early intervention services, having done so for the last 12 months.

JJ was given the Bayley-4 Cognitive scale by the clinic psychologist. His behaviors and late arrival to clinic precluded administering the motor or language scales on this visit.

The infant's chronologic age was 27 months, 20 days at the time of testing.

Level I

- The digital capture indicated that JJ's corrected age was 24 months 6 days (correction for cognitive function is recommended to extend through 2 years except for those born <25 weeks gestation where cognitive correction should extend to at least age 3) (Aylward, 2019).
- JJ received a cognitive scaled score of 5. The resultant Cognitive Composite score was 75 (5th percentile; 95% CI = 69–85). This score falls in the very low (or borderline) range with an age equivalent of 17 months.
- JJ displays a 29% delay in his cognitive abilities (i.e., 17 months/24 months = 0.71 {rounded}).

Level II

- Comparisons to other scales cannot be made at this time.
- ASD indicators were negative.

Level III

- JJ did not meet the initial basal criteria and had to begin at the next earliest start point. He was able to imitate on most occasions, receiving scores of 1 or 2. His problem-solving skills were weak (e.g., circumvents an obstacle to obtain a desired object, relational play), with JJ receiving scores of 0. Object permanency was variable, sometimes falling in the emerging category, while at other times not being present. This finding is suggestive of working memory (early executive function) weaknesses. His attempts at completing form boards were of a trial-and-error nature and mastery was elusive. This profile is congruent with the youngster's perinatal history, although a stimulating environment may lessen the negative impact of some of these historical events. Nonetheless, given that 35%–55% of children with a Grade III IVH have some type of neurodevelopmental sequelae (usually of a motoric nature), there is a good chance the insult would also affect the development of more distant brain circuits responsible for higher order processing. The EPT gestational age status also increases the likelihood of disruption in brain development. In such situations, administration of the motor subscales is important because motor functions are more directly related to medical-biological factors than to environmental ones. Furthermore, they may provide early indicators of related cognitive deficits (see Chapter 1). In addition, language subscales would also provide information relevant to overall cognitive function.

- Given the presence of IVH Grade 3, a return visit with administration of the Bayley-4 Motor and Language scales in the near future is strongly recommended.
- The Adaptive scale would also provide useful information.
- EI services already being provided should be augmented with developmental therapy.

CHAPTER 4
Language scale

Contents

Language is a complex, multifaceted developmental domain that impacts numerous related functions such as academic achievement and social skills and interactions. Language problems are relatively common, with prevalence estimates ranging from 3% to 7%, depending on age and definition (Bishop, Snowling, Thompson, Greenhalgh, CATALISE-2 Consortium, 2017). Language is typically dichotomized into expressive and receptive functioning and includes separate, yet interdependent, components such as phonology, grammar, semantics, and pragmatics (Vohr, 2014). It develops as a series of hierarchically organized skills with later higher order functions building on a base of earlier, more simple skills (Bornstein, Hahns, Putnick, & Suwalsky, 2014). One of the major conundrums in the assessment of young children with poor early language skills is determination of whether the problem is due to a delay (that implies "catch-up"), or if the subpar level of speech/language functioning is reflective of a more permanent, long-term deficit or disability. Stated differently, it is not clear if the current developmental trajectory in a child with poor speech/language skills will improve and approximate that of the typically developing child over time, or if it is a more permanent deviation.

Children who do not produce any words at 15 months of age are at risk, but typically have better outcomes than those who fail to combine words by 24 months (Rudolph & Leonard, 2016). This suggests a delay in

Bayley 4 Clinical Use and Interpretation
https://doi.org/10.1016/B978-0-12-817754-9.00004-0

the former and an increasing likelihood of a deficit or disorder in the latter. The prognosis for later language function is also poor for children with comprehension problems or those who do not use gestures. These children most likely have what is now termed a Developmental Language Disorder (formerly called a Specific Language Impairment). This new designation is compatible with ICD-11 and DSM-5 (Bishop et al., 2017).

Children produce their first words at approximately 1 year of age and increase their vocabulary gradually, by approximately one to –two words per week. Once the vocabulary expands to approximately 50 words, the pace accelerates dramatically to 1–2 new words per day (Feldman, 2019). This burst in language corresponds to myelination of white matter language pathways. With respect to additional brain development, mirror neurons (activated when the child performs an action or observes someone else performing the same action) are clustered in areas implicated in language use and these neurons are assumed to relate speech perception and actual production (Feldman, 2019).

Receptive communication

Overview

The Receptive Communication scale consists of 42 items; several new items were added and others modified. New tasks or modifications were included that: (a) allow credit for a lower criterion number of items passed, or (b) make the pass criteria easier (e.g., points to two doll body parts, points to parts of child's own or caretaker's body, versus pointing to a larger number of doll's body parts). This approach allows items to be more compatible with the framework of mastery and emerging skills.

Items were deleted based on: (a) item overlap either within the receptive communication subscale or between the Receptive and Expressive scale; (b) difficulty in scoring the item; (c) high correlations with other subscale items; (d) the likelihood of experiential bias (e.g., parenting style would have an impact on Bayley-III "inhibitory words" or "no-no"); and (e) redundancy.

The environment has a major impact on receptive and expressive language development. Hart and Risley (1995) underscored the importance of the environment in a landmark study where children were followed for 2½ years (7–9 months to 36 months) with monthly in-home observations. At age 3, children were grouped into those with a large vocabulary (~1200 words) versus those with a small vocabulary (~400–600 words). The difference between groups was related to the number of words the children had been exposed to in the home, this being linked directly to socioeconomic status (SES; SES is considered a marker variable). High SES children were estimated to be exposed to 11 million words; low SES children, 3.2 million words. By age 4, children in lower SES households were exposed to *30 million* fewer words than their high SES peers. At 9–10 years, the difference between SES groups increased, suggesting that schooling had little impact (although the quality of schooling itself may be different in a low SES milieu). In addition, lower income parents have been observed to use fewer complex sentences, ask fewer questions of children, display a paucity of sophisticated vocabulary words, and use more prohibitives and directives, versus elicit conversations (Radesky, Carta, & Bair-Merritt, 2016). The combination of these factors has led to a so-called "word gap."

However, this concept has recently been contested (Raz & Beatty, 2018), the criticisms being that the sample included only 42 families of different SES, measurement involved words spoken directly, versus the "ambient verbal environment," the difference between quality and quantity of verbal interactions was not acknowledged, and the concept of "gap" suggests a negative connotation.

Related to brain plasticity mentioned earlier, this deficit in language may also be compounded by the reports of lower family income being associated with decreased cortical surface in the frontal, temporal, and parietal areas—areas associated with vocabulary and reading (Noble, Houston, Brio, et al., 2015). Although receptive and expressive skills develop independently, both are affected by environment.

Receptive skills usually are more advanced than expressive abilities (Nazzi & Ramus, 2003). Receptively, young infants can turn their head in the general direction of a sound, with improvement in sound localization occurring over the first 6 months (Brazelton & Nugent, 2011). Over the course of the first year, infants become attuned to the overall patterns and rhythms of speech in their native languages (Jusczyk, Houston, & Newsome, 1999). They begin to respond to words and short phrases at approximately 9 months of age (Tanis-LeMonde, Bornstein, & Baumwell, 2001). Because nonlinguistic behaviors and cues displayed by the caregiver can give the impression that the child receptively understands the verbal nature of the communication, Bayley-4 items assess comprehension in the absence of contextual cues (e.g., gestures from the parent or caregiver). For example, if the child is asked to wave "bye-bye," this request should be made verbally without demonstration of the gesture because the child may simply be imitating what was seen, versus responding to what was heard. During infancy, children learn concrete linguistic expressions from the language they hear. With increased exposure and development of more complex underlying circuitry, they can creatively combine these expressions and linguistic structures in novel ways, making receptive skills necessary for the basic framework for later expressive language.

Underlying skills assessed

There are several themes that span the Receptive Communication subscale. The first is intuitive: language skills move from being simple to being more complex as the child ages. To reflect this, individual test items evaluate (in sequence) nouns, verbs, gerunds, pronouns, possessives, plurals, and past-tense verbs. Test items also move from the concrete to the abstract in terms of content. This is exemplified by the tasks evolving from pointing to objects (e.g., ball, cup; RC 16, 17), then to pictures (RC 18, 22), to displaying an understanding of concepts (e.g., size, RC 30; colors RC 34). Moving from the concrete to more abstract is also evident in the child pointing to his or her own body parts to then pointing to body parts of a doll (RC 19, 20). Learning is heavily involved with language development (Crais, 2010).

Many of the early receptive communication items involve social interaction. These include regarding a person (RC 1), calming when picked up (RC 2), responds to a voice (RC 5), responds to his or her name (RC 12), and recognition of social routines (RC 14). Although these items do not seem to be receptive communication, they should be considered significant precursors of these skills. Moreover, communication is a social function. These items are also useful in the determination of possible autism spectrum disorders.

Higher order cognitive processes are involved in the learning and application of concepts. These include sizes (RC 30), colors (RC 34), and concepts such as most, less, and mass (RC 38, 42, and 41, respectively). There is some overlap with the Cognitive scale with regard to several concepts (e.g., colors). This exemplifies the difficulty parsing a specific skill or function and placing it in only one domain, particularly in young children. Verbal working memory is assessed by the child's comprehension of one-part commands to more complex tasks such as following directions that involve prepositions (RC 31).

The Receptive Communication scale should not be used in isolation, but instead be utilized in conjunction with the Expressive Communication scale to produce the Language Composite and to allow for discrepancy comparisons. It would also be informative to compare the receptive scaled score with the Cognitive scaled score.

There are several test items that are pertinent to autism spectrum disorder (Chapter 8). These include the infant not calming when spoken to (RC 2), not responding to name being called (RC 12), does not react to caregiver (RC 6), does not attend to play routines (RC 15), or understand pronouns (RC 35).

Expressive communication

Overview

The Expressive Communication subscale contains 37 items. Items were deleted based on: (a) construct overlap (e.g., undifferentiated nasal sounds vs undifferentiated vocalizations); (b) redundancy with receptive communication subtests (e.g., responds to request for social routine); (c) two or more items could be combined into one test item (e.g., combining consonants and vowels); or (d) high correlations between items.

The Expressive subscale (as well as the Receptive) is classified as "Communication." This is particularly relevant with the expressive scale because it measures prelinguistic vocalizations, gestures, gaze, and solicitation of attention by the infant—all of which underscore the fact that communication can occur without the use of spoken "language" per se. Caregiver report is particularly helpful with expressive communication, because this is an area where refusals occur frequently due to the unfamiliar situation. In fact, this subtest has the highest number of caregiver-report questions. Items are arranged in terms of what is expected in typical language development and language milestones are also included.

Underlying skills assessed

Social interaction is prominent in the initial expressive subtests, these measuring early mutual engagement and reciprocity. Items begin with early, nonspecific vocalizations (EC 1) and progress to expression of mood and laughter (EC 3, 4), solicitation of attention (EC 6), and initiation of play and social interactions (EC 14). Socialization and communication are highly interrelated even in infancy, and this is also evident in the DSM-5 criteria for autism spectrum disorders, where persistent deficits in social interaction and communication are one of the two major diagnostic requirements.

Items progress to production of more sophisticated sounds such as vowels (EC 5), consonants (EC 7), vowel/consonant combinations (EC 8), and expressive vocalizations (10). Babbling represents the infant's active experimentation with newly acquired units of language and reciprocal social feedback to the infant's babbling facilitates more rapid phonological learning (Goldstein & Schwade, 2008). Infants imitate what they hear, modify their vocalizations based on feedback, and gradually learn to produce new sounds and combinations. More advanced nonverbal communication is also assessed via gestures (EC 9), other indicators of joint attention (e.g., EC 12), and more complex verbal and nonverbal communication combined (i.e., word + gesture; EC 19). Gestures, another form of expressive communication, differ from manual signs because they are not components of a complete language system. Children who produce the first gesture and word combinations typically are also the first to produce two-word combinations (Iverson & Goldin Meadow, 2005).

The development of vocabulary skills is also measured. This progression starts with one-word approximations (EC 11) and then involves more complex items such as imitating words (EC 13, 22), accurate word usage (15), and naming objects and pictures (EC 18, 20). Stringing words together in sentences of increasing length and complexity is the next developmental step (EC 23, 25). Articulation milestones are also included (EC 17, 24).

The toddler's ability to answer questions is found on the Bayey-4 (EC 32); however, this involves both receptive and expressive skills because the child needs to understand the question in order to answer it. Subsequently, the child is observed to pose questions (EC 28)—both of these tasks require more complex brain circuitry. Similarly complex in terms of content are tasks that involve the use of verbs and verbs with "-ing" (EC 29). Being able to express concepts (e.g., colors, possessives, prepositions, and object use; EC 34, 33, 36, 35) also requires higher order processing. The brain functions underlying these developments involve experience-expectant and experience-dependent synapses (see Chapter 1).

With regard to ASD indicators, *absence* of the following language-related behaviors raise concern: social smile (EC 2), social vocalizations (e.g., laughs; EC 3, 4), elicits attention (EC 6, 14), uses gestures (19), jabbers, imitates (words, play; 13, 22), displays joint attention (EC 12), uses gestures and words (EC 19), or answering or asking questions (EC 28, 32). Isolated findings are not overly concerning; however, the greater the number of indicators, the greater the need to investigate this area of concern (see Chapter 8).

Scoring and interpretation

Scoring levels are similar to those found in the Cognitive subscale. Correction for prematurity is again necessary through age 2 years at minimum, although there is evidence that correction for language function is necessary to age 3 depending on the criteria used (e.g., 0.33 SD difference; 0.2 SD difference, etc.; Aylward, 2019).

Level I

- Presentation of Language Composite standard score (M = 100; SD = 15).
- Level of function for Composite Language Score, percentile, 95% CI
  - Extremely high (Very exceptional), > 129
  - Very high (Exceptional), 120–129
  - High Average, 110–119
  - Average, 90–109
  - Low average, 80–89
  - Very low (Borderline), 70–79
  - Extremely low, < 70
- Listing of both the Receptive Communication and Expressive Communication scaled scores and levels of functioning (M = 10; SD = 3)
  - Exceptional/extremely high, > 13
  - High Average, 12–13
  - Average, 9–11
  - Low Average, 8
  - Borderline/very low, 6–7
  - Extremely low, < 6
- Percentiles
- 95% Confidence intervals
- Percent delay (if applicable)

Level II

- Discrepancy comparisons between expressive and receptive scaled scores; comparison to cognitive scaled score and Adaptive scaled score at 0.10 or 0.05 levels (preferably the latter)
- Compare to standard scores of other domains
- Identify indicators of possible ASD from communication as well as other scales; conversely, underscore items passed that contraindicate ASD.

Level III

- Describe strengths and weaknesses based on underlying skill areas outlined in this chapter
- Relate findings to historical or demographic information suggestive of risk, particularly environment or history of hearing loss/impairment. Identify protective factors.

Case example

Suzie Q. is a 30-month, 7-day old toddler, born full-term and whose birth history is unremarkable. She has been followed intermittently by her pediatrician since birth (the family was not conscientious in that regard), but her mother now raises concerns that Suzie Q. is "not saying much." She follows one-step directions inconsistently. The toddler is able to run smoothly, jump off the floor, kick a ball, and ascend and descend stairs holding on. Overall motor milestones were grossly within normal limits, though at the high end of normal. Suzie lives with her mom and an elder brother, age 46 months who is in an early childhood program and receives speech-language intervention. The family resides in public housing and is on Medicaid.

Interpretation

Level I

Suzie received a Language Composite standard score of 75 (5th percentile; 95% CI 68–82). This score falls in the borderline/low average range. Suzie Q's Receptive Communication raw score yielded a borderline scaled score of 7 (16th percentile). She obtained an Expressive Communication scaled score of 4, which is extremely low (2nd percentile).

Her Receptive Communication age equivalent was 25 months, while Expressive Communication was at a 15-month age level. Her receptive skills were delayed by 5 months (17%), while expressive skills were delayed by 15 months (50%).

Level II

Comparison of the Receptive and Expressive scaled scores indicates a significant difference at a 0.05 level, favoring the former (1 SD). The toddler did not meet the initial basal criteria for either scale. Although both subdomains are problematic, Expressive skills are especially concerning.

With regard to ASD indicators, Suzie Q. did not understand pronouns, utilize words and gestures, and use of one-word approximations was emerging. This was verified by caregiver report. She does attempt to elicit attention from familiar adults and did imitate words on occasion. It appears that her failed items on the ASD scale were primarily due to language delays, versus ASD per se.

Level III

Relating this to historical information, language stimulation is somewhat deficient in the home due to poor environmental circumstances. Her brother also has apparent language difficulties. Her mother did not complete high school. Suzie Q's mother did not know she was pregnant until well past the first trimester and did not have good prenatal care. The child has not received any Early Intervention services. Her overall presentation suggests a language delay, primarily in expressive skills. There is the possibility of cognitive delays as well, and the Cognitive subscale would need to be administered in addition to the Motor and Adaptive scales. These were not administered on the first evaluation due to the emergent nature of the language concerns. A hearing evaluation is also recommended, as is Speech/language EI intervention with a plan to transition to an Early Childhood Education program at age 3 years.

CHAPTER 5

Motor scale

Contents

Fine motor

Overview

The Bayley-4 Fine Motor Scale contains 46 items. In addition to eliminating and/or combining a number of Bayley-III fine motor tasks, five new developmental tasks were also added to lower test floors at specific ages.

We now understand that motor development follows a predictable sequence, but the manner and rate in which a given infant progresses through this sequence vary. Motor development is not as internally driven and unaffected by external factors as was once thought (Case-Smith & Alexander, 2010). Sensory, perceptual, and biomechanical aspects of motor function allow infants and toddlers to explore the world around them resulting in learning. This exposure reinforces experience-expectant and experience-dependent synaptic development. In motor development, there are a series of steps in which there is stability in the achievement of an ability (essentially a plateau) followed by a transition phase that occurs prior to the development of a more advanced skill. Acknowledgment of this transition stage is another reason why the Bayley-4 includes a scoring option for "emergent" skills. Gross motor abilities are affected by the infant's size, weight, coordination, ability to deal with antigravity input, strength, and maturation; fine motor abilities involve visual perceptual skills, distal maturation, cognition, size of the infant's hands, and visual-motor integration.

Bayley 4 Clinical Use and Interpretation
https://doi.org/10.1016/B978-0-12-817754-9.00005-2

The corticospinal tract (CST) is the principal motor control pathway for skilled movements (Lemon, 2008). Children rely on bilateral CST control at 6–12 months, after which a predominantly contralateral projection is established. The ipsilateral (same side) circuits are gradually eliminated and contralateral (cross-hemispheric) connectivity becomes increasingly dominant as these connections stabilize. This is evident in the infant's reaching behaviors. However, in conditions such as hemiplegic CP, the child maintains the ipsilateral CST projections from the nonaffected side, and the contralateral projections are weak (Martin, Chakrabarty, & Friel, 2011) as seen on items such as FM 11 and FM 12. Of note is the finding that motor delay is typically the first indicator of global developmental delay (Noritz, Murphy, & Neuromotor Screening Expert Panel, 2013). Moreover, primitive reflexes must cease before voluntary motor skills can be demonstrated.

Recent studies have indicated that motor development in infancy is related to cognitive function at age 4 years (Heineman, Schendelaar, Van Den Heuvel, & Hadders-Algra, 2018). Using the Infant Motor Profile at 4, 10, and 18 months of age, and the K-ABC-II at age 4, these investigators found that different aspects of motor function were related to IQ at varying ages. For example, the infants' motor repertoire (variation), adaptation (motor planning), and performance (milestones) were particularly predictive. Infants with slow motor development had a nine-point IQ decrement (0.6 SD) when compared to those with normal motor development. It appears that selecting motor strategies (adaptation) relies on the same neural networks that are also involved in cognitive tasks (executive function) (Veldman, Santos, Jones, Sousa-Sa, & Okely, 2019). Milestones (performance) or age of attainment of motor acquisitions in infancy are inversely related to intellectual function. This motor-cognitive relationship is assumed to reflect the overall integrity of established cortical-subcortical circuits (Heineman et al., 2018).

Underlying skills that are assessed

Early fine motor items involve visual tracking with emphasis placed on size of the object that is tracked (adult in the room, pencil; FM 1, 7) as well as the complexity of the tracking movement (from horizontal to vertical; FM 2, 3). Visual focus is assessed by the infant looking at a small pellet (FM 14). These skills are important because eye tracking and visual exploration are early means of experiencing the environment. Tracking across midline is a major developmental acquisition and is necessary for the development of eye-hand coordination and other more complicated abilities. Although circular tracking with the eyes was deleted, a more complex skill, namely, turning the head to the ring (which involves coordination of visual tracking and gross motor abilities), was retained (FM 6).

Sensorimotor behaviors and reflexes are also assessed at young ages; these include bringing hands to mouth (FM 4), having hands predominantly open (FM 8), displaying a palmar grasp reflex (9), or being able to rotate the wrist (FM 10, now called distal rotation). Refinement in reaching is assessed and evolves from involvement of the trunk, to use of two hands, to reaching with one hand without trunk movement. Presence of a voluntary grasp allows this progression to extend to involve inanimate objects such as retaining a ring, reaching and grasping a suspended ring (FM 11), reaching for a block, and transferring from hand to hand (ring and then block; FM 16). Refinement in type of grasp is also assessed by observing how the child manipulates blocks, or subsequently, smaller pellets (e.g., FM 13, 18, 19). These variations in grasp range from: (a) use of the entire hand; (b) thumb and finger use; to (c) a neat pincer grasp. Functional application of the fine motor skill of grasping is also assessed by the infant putting pellets in a bottle or stringing small blocks on a shoelace (FM 25, 36). These tasks, as well as putting coins in a bank (FM 27), require more refined precision, manipulation, and placement skills.

Use of standard 1-in. blocks in increasingly more difficult tasks is also a major skill set. Tasks involving blocks range from stacking increasing numbers of blocks t (FM 24, 30, 33) to building simple structures such as a train or a bridge (FM 35, 38). These tests require recruitment of various skills such as precision grasp, release, stability of arm in space, visual perception, and the capacity to modulate motor skills in response to kinesthetic and proprioceptive feedback.

Similarly, the development of writing skills is assessed; this involving functional use of objects. The first area of assessment is evaluation of how the pencil is grasped. The type of grasp proceeds from palmar, transitional, static tripod, to dynamic (FM 21, 26, 29, 45). The second array of writing items involves actual production. Visual perception, fine motor control, and visual-motor integration are necessary for successful scribbling (FM 23), imitating strokes (e.g., 40, 42), and subsequently *imitating* more complex figures such as a circle, plus sign, and square. The more complex tasks of *tracing and then copying* figures such as a plus sign or a square follow (e.g., FM 43, 46). The latter is the most difficult copying task on the Bayley-4. These tasks also require perceptual skills and visual-motor planning. Examiners should remember that imitation is evident before actual copying of a figure.

There is also a potpourri of additional fine motor items that are not easily grouped, but which serve to provide a more complete, overall assessment of the child's fine motor abilities. Some items assess application of fine motor skills such as the toddler being able to self-feed finger foods (FM 17) turn pages of a book (FM 20), connect and then disconnect blocks (28, 32), and fold paper (FM 37). Fine motor speed and coordination are necessary for finger tapping (FM 44), which is one of the most difficult fine motor tasks.

Gross motor

The Bayley-4 Gross motor subtest contains 58 items; new items include primitive reflexes (or their absence; e.g., GM 12,19), protective reflexes (GM 9, 14), and several gross motor items such as rolling from stomach to back or jumping off the floor with both feet leaving the surface simultaneously (GM 48).

Gross motor skills include head control, trunk control, locomotion, and motor planning. The infant and toddler's ability to move about the environment has a significant impact on other areas of development. As was indicated in Chapter 1, regarding upper and lower motor control systems (Amiel-Tison & Gosselin, 2008), primitive reflexes become less prominent (e.g., ATNR; GM 12) and protective reactions appear (GM 9, 14), as do postural reactions and more purposeful movements. Postural stability and control in terms of balance when stationary and during movement (dynamic) is another major developmental acquisition that is assessed (GM 30, 32, 33, 36).

Head control is an extremely important function and involves a balance of neck extension and flexion. Good head control is necessary for the infant to engage the environment. On the Bayley-4, head control is assessed when the infant is held upright, then subsequently if the infant can lift his head from side to side when prone. Control in supine and prone suspensions (dorsal, ventral) reveals flexor and extensor strength and control as does righting the head in reaction to change in orientation while held in a vertical suspension (GM 2–6, 8, 15, 18). Various stages of volitional head lifting are observed and measured while the infant is prone; the most advanced being the infant raising her head 90 degrees from the surface (GM 15). Poor head control, in general, is traditionally considered an early indicator of neuromotor problems and raises significant concerns.

Sitting depends on truncal tone (as well as head control) and items that involve sitting range from sitting supported to sitting without support, both over increasingly longer durations of time (GM 13, 16, 24). Mobility is a key skill that allows the child to explore the environment and includes rolling over, pivoting, crawling on stomach, and crawling on hands and knees (e.g., GM 26, 29).

Dynamic postural stability is necessary for walking and standing. This is first evident in the infant showing early stepping movements (GM 25) and then supporting his or her weight (GM 28). Raising oneself to a standing position by use of a chair, walking with support, walking sideways, the infant standing with his back straight, and standing without support are additional Bayley-4 items that evaluate postural stability (GM 30–32). Sitting down with control (versus plopping on one's rump; GM 33), standing up alone, and displaying an unsupported squatting maneuver (GM 38) are examples of motor modulation of antigravity muscles. More advanced coordination, motor control, balance, and motor sequencing skills are assessed with items such as running, stopping short from a full run, hopping, walking backwards, heel to toe walking, or kicking a ball (e.g., GM 40, 42, 51, 53, 55). Standing on one foot with and without support measures balance (43, 49). Throwing a ball (37), jumping off the floor, off the bottom step, and forwards (e.g., GM 44, 47, 48), and purposeful tiptoe walking round out the stability items and require a combination of tone, balance, stability, and coordination in their execution.

Stair items that involve both the manner of ascent and descent (i.e., both feet on each step (marching), versus alternating feet on each step), as well as the need for support (GM 39, 41, 52) are another series of skills that are evaluated. These gross motor items involve balance, antigravity movements, muscle strength, and motor planning.

To summarize, neural and developmental factors contribute to adequate or abnormal muscle tone. For example, the basal ganglia often are involved in increased muscle tone (hypertonia), while the cerebellum is associated with low tone (hypotonia) (Goo, Tucker, & Johnston, 2018).

On the Bayley-4 gross motor subscale, muscle activation versus muscle tone in the resting state is assessed, initially in the head and neck and upper limbs; the infant's ability to recruit postural muscles (active postural tone) in an effort to maintain a part of the body against gravity is evaluated. Other items such as cuddliness when held by the caregiver measure overall muscle tone, particularly the ability to relax active muscles. Many gross motor items contain other transitional dimensions that reflect the infant's ability to respond to changes in external demands (Goo et al., 2018).

Scoring and interpretation

The approach to scoring is similar to that found in Cognitive and Language function.

Level I

- Record the standard score for the Motor Composite (M = 100, SD = 15).
- Percentile
- 95% confidence interval
- Level of function for Motor Composite score:
  - Extremely high/Very exceptional (> 129)
  - Very high/Exceptional (120–129)
  - High average (110–119)
  - Average (90–109)
  - Low average (80–89)
  - Very low/Borderline (70–79)
  - Extremely low (< 70)
- Scaled scores for the Fine and Gross motor subscales (M = 10, SD = 3) should be recorded and level of function of scaled scores is selected from the following:
  - Very high/Exceptional, > 13
  - High average, 12–13
  - Average, 9–11
  - Low average, 8
  - Very low/Borderline, 6–7
  - Extremely low, < 6
- Age equivalents of fine and gross motor subdomains.
- Percent delay (if applicable)

Level II

- Discrepancy comparisons between fine and gross motor scaled scores at a 0.10 or 0.05 level (preferably the latter)
- Comparison with standard scores of other domains

Level III

- Describe strengths and weaknesses in each subdomain, based on underlying skill areas outlined in this chapter.
- Discuss any abnormal indicators (e.g., cortical thumb, persistent tonic neck posturing, abnormalities in tone) (Chapter 10).

- Relate findings to environmental or biomedical history, with realization that motor function is more directly related to medical/biological risk factors than environmental ones. Also note that motor function has more of a self-righting tendency than do cognitive abilities (Aylward, 2009).

Case example

Wally is a 12-month-old born at term who displayed evidence of hypoxic ischemic encephalopathy (HIE), and as a result, was placed on a total body cooling protocol at 3 hours of age. Blood pH was <7.1, respiration was delayed, he was lethargic and unresponsive, and his 5-minute Apgar was 4. The 10-minute Apgar score was 5. He was placed on anticonvulsant medication in the neonatal unit because of suspected seizures, and, despite this series of events, was discharged 9 days after birth. Wally's parents were told that he had neonatal encephalopathy by an attending neonatologist. No MRI was done. His milestones were reported to be delayed early on, with persistence of primitive reflexes.

Interpretation

Level I

Wally obtained a Motor Composite standard score of 63 (0.1 percentile; 95% confidence interval 56–70). This score falls in the extremely low range. Wally's Fine Motor raw score equated to a scaled score of 5 (2nd percentile), while the raw score on the Gross motor subscale produced a scale score of 1 (<1st percentile). Wally's fine motor skills were at a 6-month age level (50% delay), while gross motor abilities were at a 4-month age equivalent (66%) delay.

Level II

There was a statistically significant difference between the fine and gross motor scores at a 0.10 level (but not at 0.05).

With respect to underlying skill groupings, sensorimotor abilities were often deficient or, at best, emerging. This suggests significant impairment. When Wally reached for a block he did not touch it consistently, he reached with both hands, and his capacity to grasp and retain blocks was variable. Midline behaviors were emerging and he could transfer a ring from one hand to the other, but could not do so with a block. Wally was reported to have difficulty visually tracking objects across the midline when he was tested informally at a younger age.

When held under his armpits, he displayed "slip through," indicating decreased tone in the shoulders. Wally does not right his head equally in all orientations when held vertically. He leans forward when sitting and does not make stepping movements; instead, he locks out his legs in extension and bends at the waist when placed upright on the exam table. He is reported to occasionally try to pull himself up to standing using his parents' pant legs, but typically is not successful. The infant has begun crawling on his hands and knees only within the last month. From these findings, it appears that head control, trunk control, and tone are problematic and there is no dynamic postural stability at this time. Occasional scissoring was noted in the downwards parachute item.

Level III

Significant neurodevelopmental disabilities are found in 25% of infants with neonatal encephalopathy attributable to HIE, although therapeutic hypothermia reduces death or disability in comparison to infants with HIE who do not receive such by several percentage points (Laptook et al., 2017). Wally appears to have sustained CNS insult. The hypotonia and history of persistence of primitive reflexes with aberrant protective reactions are worrisome and raise the possibility of a significant neuromotor disorder (CP). Without doubt, the infant will need OT and PT Early Intervention services. Wally will need to have the Bayley-4, Cognitive, Language, and Adaptive scales administered to determine if he has a global developmental delay. The infant's hearing should be evaluated because this is a frequent sequela of birth asphyxia.

CHAPTER 6

Adaptive Behavior Scale

Contents

Overview

The Adaptive Behavior Scale contains items and skill areas derived from the Comprehensive Parent/Caregiver Form of the Vineland Adaptive Behavior Scales, Third Edition (Sparrow, Cicchetti, & Saulnier, 2016). The Adaptive Behavior Scale enables assessment of the child's daily functional skills by measuring what he or she does *routinely*, in contrast to what he or she may be *capable* of doing.

Adaptive, functional skills are necessary for the child to become more independent. Adaptive behavior is age-related and broadens in scope co-inciding with increasing age and development. Adaptive behaviors are modifiable—much more so than other developmental domains such as cognitive abilities. It must be emphasized that adaptive behaviors on the Vineland-3 (and on the Bayley-4) are defined by *typical performance*, not *ability or capacity to do a task*. Although the child may be capable of demon-strating a behavior, the behavior must be translated into regular, day-to-day

Bayley 4 Clinical Use and Interpretation
https://doi.org/10.1016/B978-0-12-817754-9.00006-4

implementation. Stated differently, adaptive behavior reflects what the child typically does in daily interactions with the environment; if the toddler has the capacity to do a task but does not do it routinely, this behavior is not considered adaptive. Moreover, the behaviors should occur independently and without assistance or prompting.

Adaptive behaviors on the Bayley-4 are measured solely via caregiver report because self- or teacher-report obviously cannot be obtained for children in this age range. Potential negative issues regarding parent completion of the Adaptive Behavior Scale include problems with comprehension of items and underreporting/overreporting (deliberate or unintentional). However, the tendency to over- or underreport should also be evident from caregiver report responses obtained over the course of the administration of the other Bayley-4 scales.

In agreement with Diagnostic and Statistical Manual of Mental Disorders Fifth Edition (DSM-5; American Psychiatric Association, 2013) and the American Association on Intellectual and Developmental Disabilities (AAIDD, 2010), the infant's adaptive skills are considered to be a reflection of underlying cognitive, motor, language, and social-emotional functioning. It is assumed that the significance or effect of deficits in these streams of developmental function will ultimately be apparent in the quality of the child's adaptive abilities. Stated differently, adaptive skills gauge the functional impact of problems in the basic areas of development on the child's day-to-day dealings with environmental demands.

Impairment, handicap, and disability

The World Health Organization defines *Impairment* as a loss or abnormality of a psychological, physiological, or anatomical structure or function. A *Disability* is a restriction in the ability to perform a function that is the result of an impairment. A *Handicap* is defined as a disadvantage that results when a disability or impairment limits or prevents a child from doing a task or displaying a function. If a child has a disability, but can display adaptive behavior in response to environmental demands, albeit in an unconventional manner, credit should be given on the Adaptive Behavior Scales. A simple example would be the usage of signs to "say" something.

Why emphasize functional skills?

Much of the impetus for assessment of functional skills comes from the most recent update of IDEA (2004). This law originally was named The Education for All Handicapped Children Act (94-142; 1975), which then evolved into the Individuals with Disabilities Act (99-457, 1986). Part C involves Early Intervention (birth to age 3); Part B is applicable from ages 3 to 21. With regard to the Bayley-4, Part B involves Early Childhood Education (ECE). Eligibility criteria for EI services under Part C and ECE under Part B include: (1) presence of a *developmental delay* in cognitive, physical, communication, social-emotional, or *adaptive* function; (2) presence of a medical condition that is related to the high likelihood of a developmental delay; or (3) the infant or toddler is considered "at-risk" (Roberts & Kennert, 2018). Intervention has a family emphasis as evident in the Individual Family Service Plan (IFSP) and the fact that intervention should be provided in the child's natural environment, versus a center.

The term, developmental delay, is defined differently depending on the child's geographic location. Some states require a percent delay in one or more areas such as 20%, 25%, 30%, or even 50%. Others use combinations such as 50% delay if this occurs in only one area, but 25% delay if two or more developmental areas are involved. Some states use standard deviations below the mean (e.g., 2, 1.5, 1.4), while others employ months of delay (e.g., 6 months below the norm for the child's chronological age). Other permutations comingle age of child and percent delay, while some states have vague criteria and leave intervention decisions up to "a team of professionals." Tests typically used or not allowed to be used to qualify for EI services also vary depending on the state, further adding to the confusion.

Domains

The three domains of the Bayley-4 Adaptive Behavior Scale, namely, Communication, Daily Living Skills, and Socialization, are compatible with the adaptive behavior areas specified as necessary for the diagnosis of later intellectual disability (ID) by the American Association on Intellectual and Developmental Disabilities (AAIDD, 2010) and the Diagnostic and Statistical Manual of Mental Disorders-5 (APA, 2013). The AAIDD and DSM-5 use the terms conceptual, practical, and social, instead of the domain names, Communication, Daily Living Skills, and Socialization of the Vineland-3 (and the Bayley-4). Deficits in these areas are rated as mild, moderate, and severe, by the APA and AAIDD, reflecting the impact the adaptive skill deficit has on the individual's day-to-day function. On the Bayley-4, severity is reflected by standardized scores.

Selection of items

The Bayley-4 Adaptive Behavior Scale consists of 120 items selected from the Vineland-3 (Sparrow et al., 2016). Fifty-one items were extracted from the Receptive and Expressive subdomains (23 from the former; 28 latter) to comprise the *Communication Domain* item set. The *Daily Living Skills* item set contains 30 items from the Caring for Self-subdomain. The *Socialization Domain* includes 39 items from the Interpersonal Relationships (20) and Play and Leisure (19) subdomains. An Adaptive Behavior Composite (ABC) and subdomain scaled scores are available.

No Vineland-3 data were available for ages 0–3 years for the Written, Domestic, or Community subdomains; these were not included in the Bayley-4. No data were available for ages 0–24 months for the Coping Skills subdomain and this also was deleted. The steps in the selection of items for the Bayley-4 Adaptive scales can be found in the Bayley-4 Technical Manual (Bayley & Aylward, 2019a). The normative sample for the Adaptive Behavior Scale consisted of 759 children from 0 to 42 months of age. The comparative clinical sample was comprised of 49 children (12% ASD; 88% developmental delay).

Underlying skills assessed

Communication

This domain is comprised of two subdomains:

Receptive subdomain (listening and understanding)

The early items in this subdomain include many social-interactive components: responding to the caregiver's voice, understanding the intent of caregiver's gestures of varying complexity, response to the child's name being called, joint attention (e.g., looks at direction of caregiver's point), and understanding if the caregiver is angry based on the tone of the parent's voice. This array of items is also useful in evaluating a child suspected of having autism spectrum disorder and can supplement information from the ASD Checklist.

The child's understanding of words is another skill area found in this subdomain. This capacity is assessed via the toddler pointing to pictures or objects named by an adult, following directions of increasing complexity, identifying body parts, understanding words, and answering increasingly complex questions.

At older ages, verbal memory and attention come into play as measured by being able to listen to a story, or if told to do something at one point and later on the toddler remembers to do it.

Expressive subdomain (talking)

The initial items also are social in nature, such as making sounds to solicit attention or use gestures. Prelanguage skills such as making short speech sounds, babbling, and saying "dada" or "mama" are also included.

Vocabulary development comprises the bulk of this subdomain and includes:

- Naming objects
- Repeating words
- Making one-word requests
- Describing actions
- Having a 50-word vocabulary
- Able to say first and last name, age
- Noun/verb combinations and then more complex sentences
- Plurals, pronouns, possessives, adjectives, prepositions
- Uses past tense
- Answers questions

Verbal memory is again assessed with the child being able to tell parts of a story or time events.

Daily living skills

This area is comprised of one subdomain:

Caring for self-subdomain

This subdomain addresses the child's ability to care for himself or herself during activities of daily living. These activities include eating, drinking, and increasing levels of difficulty with regard to dressing and undressing. Other activities involve toileting, washing, brushing teeth, and more specific behaviors such as the child blowing his or her nose or covering the mouth or nose when coughing or sneezing.

Socialization

The Socialization domain contains two subdomains:

Interpersonal relationships (relating to others)

Earlier items involve caregiver-child interactions: the infant smiles, reaches for the caregiver, shows affection, and makes eye contact. The second area of function describes the toddler's interest in other children, imitation, and ability to recognize the emotions of others. The last adaptive area assesses the toddler's friendships. This subdomain also is particularly informative if the question of Autism Spectrum Disorder is raised.

Play and leisure (playing)

Playing begins with simple games with the caregiver such as peek-a-boo or patty cake and evolves into playing with other children. Playing with peers, the ability to move from parallel playing to sharing, and asking for things possessed by others (versus simply taking them) are also rated. Playing make-believe games and engaging in group activities, including taking turns, are part of this subdomain.

Scoring and interpretation

A frequency-based response scale is used. If the behavior under consideration *usually* occurs, a score of "2" is given. If the behavior occurs *sometimes*, the score is "1." Absence of the behavior (*never*) warrants a score of "0." This format is similar to the polytomous scoring employed in the Bayley-4 Cognitive, Language, and Motor scales. There is also an option to check off "estimated" if the adult completing the scale is not certain as to the frequency of the particular adaptive behavior. If the number of estimated responses is <15%, then the report is most likely valid. If the percentage is ≥ 15% but < 25%, caution should be exercised in interpretation; however, if estimated responses are ≥ 25%, the usefulness of report is called to question.

Scores for the overall Bayley Adaptive Behavior Composite (ABC) and three Domain scores (M = 100, SD = 15; range 20–140) are derived. Five subdomain scores provide scaled scores with a mean of 10 and SD of 3. Age equivalents are also available for the five subdomains.

General: Correct for prematurity up to age 2 years.

Level I

- Record the Adaptive Behavior Composite score
- Percentile
- 95% confidence interval
- Five subdomain scaled scores and age equivalents
- Three standard scores for the Communication, Daily Living Skills, and Socialization Domains and percentiles
- Percent delay (if appropriate)

Level II

- Discrepancies between the three subdomains
- Comparison with other Bayley-4 composite scores

Level III

- Describe strengths and weaknesses
- Relate findings to child's history
- Discuss any pathognomonic indicators (red flags) including those linked with ASD.

Case example

Sammy is a 36-month toddler who is being evaluated because his pediatrician believes that the youngster needs to be enrolled in an Early Childhood program. His parents are ambivalent about this possibility. The preschooler had received Early Intervention services previously: developmental therapy, speech/language therapy, and physical therapy. Sammy's parents often did not follow-through on the therapists' recommendations.

Sammy's pediatrician raises significant concerns regarding the youngster's communication skills and possibly ASD. His vocabulary is limited, he doesn't seem to understand verbal directions, cannot provide answers to questions in a consistent fashion, produces simple sentences, and is unable to recount parts of a story read to him. Sammy seems to have no difficulty with regard to eating or dressing, but needs supervision washing, brushing his teeth, and toileting. He likes to play with other children, especially his cousins who are of similar ages. Tag, hide and seek, and similar games are his favorites.

Interpretation

Level I

Sammy was given the full Bayley-4. He received an Adaptive Behavior Composite of 81 (10th percentile; ±4). This falls in the low average to borderline range. Sammy's Receptive subdomain scaled score was 6 (9th percentile), and the Expressive score, 5 (5th percentile). The Communication Domain standard score was 75 (5th percentile; 95% CI = ±5), this falling in the very low or borderline range. The Personal Domain scale score was 8 (25th percentile) and the resultant Daily Living Skills standard score was 90 (25th percentile; ±8) which is average. The Interpersonal relationships subdomain scaled score was 8, (25th percentile) while the Play and Leisure standard score was 9 (37th percentile). Sammy's resultant Socialization standard score was 91 (27th percentile; 95% CI = ±6).

Level II

The difference between the preschooler's Communication and both the Daily Living Skills and Socialization Domains is significant (0.05) and reflects strengths in Sammy's self-care and social-interactive adaptive functioning. Conversely, his Communication skills are an area of relative weakness.

Level III

The overall Adaptive Behavior Composite of 81 and the identified strengths and weaknesses were found to be in line with Sammy's other Bayley-4 scores. More specifically, he received a Cognitive Composite score of 78 (7th percentile), a Language Composite of 68 (2nd percentile), and a Motor Composite of 86 (16th percentile). Taken together, the main area of weakness is language, with other functional domains being low average to borderline. Whether these skills are emerging or Sammy will continue to remain behind peers will become more evident over time. No cause for the language problems could be identified, although there does appear to be a positive family history of "late talkers." Sammy will need to be enrolled in an Early Childhood classroom with specific help in language development. More specific testing by a speech/language pathologist is recommended, as is a hearing evaluation.

CHAPTER 7

Social-Emotional Scale

Contents

Overview

The Social-Emotional Scale is basically unchanged from the Bayley-III, being a norm-referenced adaptation of the "Greenspan Social-Emotional Growth Chart: A Screening Questionnaire for Infants and Young Children" (Greenspan, 2004, Greenspan & Shanker, 2004). Similar to Adaptive functioning, acquisition of social and emotional milestones in infants and young children is assessed via caregiver report. This is accomplished in the context of identifying the major social-emotional developmental milestones that should be mastered by certain ages.

A distinction is made between *specific emotions or social skills* and the *acquisition of functional emotional milestones* (Breinbauer, Mancil, & Greenspan, 2010; Greenspan, 1989, 1997; Greenspan, DeGangi, & Wieder, 2001; Greenspan & Shanker, 2004). Functional emotional milestones focus on larger, more cohesive emotional patterns that define typical emotional functioning. They are not isolated emotions per se. These milestones include the capacity to engage others with a range of emotions (e.g., joyful intimacy, assertiveness); to experience, express, and comprehend a variety of emotional signals; and

Bayley 4 Clinical Use and Interpretation
https://doi.org/10.1016/B978-0-12-817754-9.00007-6

to elaborate a range of feelings with words and symbols (e.g., pretend play) (Breinbauer et al., 2010).

Underlying areas assessed

Based on the functional emotional milestones identified by Greenspan, six stages (with two additional substages) are identified for children from birth to 42 months of age. These milestones and relevant ages are:

- Stage 1: Infant shows growing self-regulation and interest in the world (0–3 months)
- Stage 2: Child engages in relationships (4–5 months)
- Stage 3: Child uses emotions in an interactive, purposeful manner (6–9 months)
- Stage 4a: Child uses a series of interactive emotional signals or gestures to communicate (10–14 months)
- Stage 4b: Toddler employs a series of interactive emotional signals or gestures to solve problems (15–18 months)
- Stage 5a: Child uses symbols or ideas to convey intentions or feelings (19–24 months)
- Stage 5b: Uses symbols or ideas to express more than basic needs (25–30 months)
- Stage 6: Creates logical bridges between emotions and ideas (31–42 months)

In addition, there is an eight-item sensory processing section that documents the child's hyper- or hypo-reactivity to visual, auditory, and tactile stimulation, as well as body movement.

At age 5 months and below, the child's ability to engage in preliminary social interactions and awareness of his or her environment are assessed. Self-regulatory behaviors (e.g., is able to calm down with help) and interest in the infant's expanding world are evaluated (visual and auditory), as are sensory capacities. Relationships with familiar persons are developed.

By 6–9 months, the infant solicits social interactions, and emotions are purposefully involved in interactions (including elements of joint attention). The social-emotional increment at 10–14 months involves the interchange of gestures and chains of communication (essentially, social reciprocity).

Preliminary use of words and a general increase in the complexity of communication occur at 15–18 months; gestures and emotional signals are utilized in day-to-day problem solving. Social reciprocity is evident. By 19–24 months, the toddler uses single words and follows commands.

These abilities reflect an expansion of receptive and expressive language skills. Pretend play also is developing.

At older ages, social-emotional growth reflects the ability to make-believe, pretend, and engage in social communication with peers (25–30 months). Emotions become more complex. The most advanced emotional stage involves make-believe activities with peers, production of more complex sentences including questions, capacity to explain wants, and to engage in extended conversations with multiple exchanges (31–42 months). Children at this age make connections between emotions expressed by themselves and others.

Sensory processing is also emphasized, the premise being that sensory processing problems will have a negative impact on social-emotional growth (Breinbauer et al., 2010). The logic behind evaluating both sensory processing and social-emotional functioning measures is that these have a reciprocal relationship; each influences the other's development (Breinbauer et al., 2010). For example, disturbances of sensory processing could have an impact on social-emotional responses and expressions in the form of overreactivity to what would seem totally innocuous to most children of the same age (e.g., visual or auditory); or conversely, underreactivity to sensory input that typically developing infants and toddlers would respond to or perhaps find aversive.

The social-emotional form is filled out by respondents familiar with the infant or toddler, namely, parents or a primary caregiver. An interview is not necessary. Strengths include ease of administration, a format to assess this area of functioning at young ages, and inclusion of the sensory processing component. Perhaps, one of the more unique components is the Social-Emotional Growth Chart that can be used as a surveillance instrument (see p. 13 of the Social-Emotional and Adaptive Behavior Questionnaire). Professionals can monitor the child's rate of progress as: (1) faster than expected; (2) slower progress than expected; or (3) increasing social-emotional problems with age. Regression or early onset of social-emotional problems can also be detected.

On the Social-Emotional form, scoring for all infants and toddlers begins on item number 1. The caregiver is requested to stop scoring the scale when the stop point, based on the child's age, is reached. There are eight such stop points. There is no ceiling based on the number of items scored "1" (none of the time). If the respondent cannot rate an item, "can't tell" (0) is selected. If > 15% of the responses fall in this category, the results should be interpreted cautiously.

Scoring and interpretation

The 35 Social-Emotional items are scored on a 0–5 scale:

- Can't tell—0
- None of the time—1
- Some of the time—2
- Half of the time—3
- Most of the time—4
- All of the time—5

Level I

- Presentation of the Social-Emotional standard score based on scaled score (1–19).
- 95% confidence interval
- Percentile rank
- Level of function
  - Very exceptional; > 129
  - Exceptional; 120–129
  - High average; 110–119
  - Average; 90–109
  - Low average; 80–89
  - Borderline; 70–79
  - Extremely low; < 70

Level II

- Determine the Sensory Processing Index score category based on cut scores
  - Possible challenges
  - Emerging mastery
  - Full mastery

Level III

- Given that social-emotional functioning is impaired in children with ASD, this should be a consideration if there are significant deficits in this area.
- Similarly, because the DSM-5 also includes sensory processing issues in the diagnosis of restricted, repetitive behaviors, these should be evaluated in relation to ASD. This information should be used in conjunction with the Bayley-4 ASD checklist.

- Differences in scaled scores between the Social-Emotional Scale and other Bayley-4 scales should be evaluated.
- There is also the aforementioned Social-Emotional Growth Chart in which normal or typical social-emotional development is indicated by a 45 degree line. A given child's performance can be compared to this standard to help determine graphically how atypical the child's social-emotional development is. The horizontal *x*-axis is the child's age in months, while the vertical *y*-axis contains the emotional stages.

Overlap in measurements

What becomes apparent when considering the five combined scales of the Bayley-4 is the overlap and interrelatedness of developmental skill sets. This is not specific to the Bayley, but rather it reflects the concept of development in general. Communication tasks are found and measured in the Language, Adaptive, and Social-Emotional Scales. Motor skills (particularly fine motor) are involved in the Motor, Adaptive (e.g., Personal), and to some degree, Cognitive scales. Social skills are also assessed on multiple scales, namely, Adaptive, Language, and Social-Emotional. Overlapping skills reflect the interrelatedness of developmental domains and the fact that they are not easily parsed during infancy and toddlerhood. Analogous to the underlying "G" and subskills found in intelligence testing, there most likely is an analogous underlying, general "D" (development) with subskills in various streams of development. This overlap may also reflect the limitations on what we can or should measure in young children. A benefit to the overlap is that it affords cross-validation of strengths and weaknesses on different measures.

Case example

Cooper is an 18-month old male whose parents are concerned regarding his social and interactive skills. He is quite fussy and has been so for most of his first year and a half. He becomes overstimulated easily, particularly by sounds that are of a moderate loudness, or when his parents take him places such as the local shopping mall with bustling activity. He often simply ignores direct, social initiatives of others by staring away from the person speaking to him. Language abilities are weak with only single word communication that is highly inconsistent and difficult to understand. Similarly, pointing and gestures are rarely noted. He has not had much opportunity to interact with peers because he spends most of his time at home with his mother. The parents finally brought these concerns up with Cooper's pediatrician, who, in turn, made a referral to the local medical school's Child Development Clinic. The developmental psychologist at the clinic administered the Bayley-4, although Cooper was not very cooperative and essentially refused to engage in most test tasks, despite a herculean effort by the examiner. Parent report was utilized when possible, but overall was not sufficient to produce a Cognitive, Language, or Motor Composite.

Scoring and interpretation

Level I

As indicated above, Cooper was essentially untestable with the Bayley-4 Cognitive, Language, or Motor scales. As a result, the evaluation consisted of observations and parent report when appropriate. Unfortunately, the number of parent report items was not sufficient to produce any scores. Cooper's parents did complete the Bayley-4 Social-Emotional and Adaptive Behavior Questionnaires and the behaviors from ASD Checklist were checked off, based on examiner observation and parent report. Cooper received a Social-Emotional Scaled score of 70 (2nd percentile; 95% CI = ±2). The cut score on the Sensory Processing scale fell in the "Possible challenges" category.

Level II

A sizeable number of items on the ASD Checklist (p. 84; Bayley-4 Technical Manual; Bayley & Aylward, 2019b) were indicated. Imitative skills were infrequent, Cooper did not use gestures regularly, deficits in joint attention were noted, and laughing was minimal. Social referencing and self-regulatory behaviors were lacking.

Results of the Adaptive Behavior Scale were compatible; the Receptive, Expressive, Personal, Interpersonal Relationships, and Play and Leisure subdomain scaled scores were at the 5th percentile or below. The resultant Composite Scores (Communication, Daily Living Skills, and Socialization) were all < 55.

Level III

Cooper demonstrates behaviors that are suggestive of possible ASD. His behaviors are atypical for a toddler his age and firm estimates of his cognitive, language, or motor skills are elusive at this time. Adaptive skills are significantly delayed and numerous items on the ASD Checklist were endorsed. The Social-Emotional and Sensory Processing scores are of concern as well. Observations during testing also were suggestive of ASD. In response, it is recommended that further evaluation with more specific ASD instruments such as the ADOS be undertaken, although much of the information will have to be gleaned from parent report and observation, as Cooper tends to not participate in interactive activities. EI services geared toward children with ASD are necessary, including speech/language, developmental therapy, and ABA. Further attempts at developmental testing should be undertaken in several months; this done in an incremental fashion.

CHAPTER 8

The Autism Spectrum Disorder Checklist

The CDC indicates that the prevalence of Autism Spectrum Disorders (ASD) in children of age 8 years is now 1/59 or 16.8 per 1000 (Baio et al., 2018), with the median age of diagnosis being 52 months. However, the proportion of children with suspected ASD who received a comprehensive developmental evaluation by age 3 years was 42%, suggesting that suspicions regarding the child not showing typical development or behavior had existed earlier. This brings up the intriguing possibility that an infant or toddler referred because of concerns in development and tested with the Bayley-4 could also be monitored for ASD. If a number of specific concerns were identified, more detailed ASD-specific screening or testing could be undertaken. In doing so, identification may be accomplished more than a year earlier than the median age at which this process is currently being completed. Earlier identification is important because there is evidence that the earlier the access to intervention, the greater the likelihood of improved outcome (Johnson, Myers, & American Academy of Pediatrics Council of Children with Disabilities, 2007).

With regard to screening per se, more than 20 ASD-specific screeners have been developed over the last several decades; however, the issue has been raised as to whether general developmental screening tools can also identify children who should then be evaluated for ASD (Wiggins, Piazza, & Robins, 2014; Zwaigenbaum et al., 2015). Data that address this issue are mixed. In the Wiggins et al.'s study, 75% of children with a positive finding on an ASD-specific screener (M-CHAT) were missed by the PEDS (Glascoe, 1998), which is a developmental screening tool. This finding raises the possibility that general developmental screeners and ASD-specific screeners may not measure the same constructs, perhaps because both types of screeners contain a limited number of items and these tend to be restricted to the specific purpose of the screener. As a result, it was suggested that, in addition to general developmental screening, autism-specific screeners should be used. Conversely, in another study comparing

Bayley 4 Clinical Use and Interpretation
https://doi.org/10.1016/B978-0-12-817754-9.00008-8

the ASQ-3 (Bricker & Squires, 2009) and the M-CHAT-R, Hardy, Haisley, Manning, and Fein (2015) reported that problems identified in the ASQ-3 developmental domain of Communication correctly identified 95% of children later diagnosed with ASD. These authors suggested use of a broadband screener first, and if it is positive, an ASD-specific screener should then be employed. Finally, in a sample of almost 19,000 children, 54% of those with both a positive M-CHAT-R and the follow-up M-CHAT/I were subsequently diagnosed with ASD. However, 98% of these children with positive M-CHAT-R/I results had significant developmental concerns (Chlebowski, Robins, Barton, & Fein, 2013). Summarizing the implications drawn from these studies, there is overlap among developmental issues and symptoms of ASD, but there are also unique components specific to developmental and ASD Checklists.

More recently, in a sample of more than 2200 children referred for evaluation of ASD after being screened by their PCP or community agency, assessments were done at a median age of 17.6 months and 36.2 months. Overall diagnostic stability for ASD was 0.84 and it was 0.79 by 14 months (0.50 at 12–13 months and 0.83 by 16 months) (Pierce et al., 2019). The authors speculate that the lower stability at 12 months is due to limitations in the diagnostic tools used at that age (ADOS-2 and DSM-5). Nonetheless, identification of children with ASD is possible at an age younger than 3–4 years, underscoring the potential benefit of a checklist that can be completed during a developmental evaluation.

Therefore, a detailed developmental evaluation (e.g., Bayley-4) that also includes a checklist of administered and observed items and parent report indicating ASD-related behaviors would be highly useful. While Level I screening is given to all children, Level II is considered targeted screening, administered to children from a population identified as already being at risk. It would appear that Level II screening is in effect when administering the Bayley-4 ASD Checklist because the developmental status of children being given the Bayley-4 most likely already is a concern. Administration of the Bayley-4 affords the opportunity to assess levels of performance in the major developmental domains, and it also contains items that raise awareness of behaviors associated with ASD. General developmental concerns and data suggestive of the need for more specific ASD evaluation can be obtained simultaneously. It is imperative to emphasize that a diagnosis of ASD cannot be made solely based on the Bayley-4 ASD Checklist and that "detection must not be mistaken for diagnosis" (Dan, 2018). Similarly, the younger the child, the less certain one can be that the behaviors are indicative of ASD, even with established screening instruments such as the M-CHAT-R (Yuen, Penner, Carter, & Szatmari, 2018). Nonetheless, the Bayley-4 ASD Checklist will help examiners flag the child who needs more frequent or detailed follow-up. This checklist is found in Appendix A of the Bayley-4 Technical Manual (pp. 83–86).

Furthermore, clinical populations have higher prevalence rates of various developmental disorders, and the disorders tend to cluster together in these populations. Because of this clustering, there most likely is a greater prevalence of ASD in children whose development is in question than in the general population. In a recent Norwegian study (Oien et al., 2018), it was reported that children who tested negative for ASD at 18 months but who were diagnosed with ASD at later ages demonstrated early delays and atypical features. These indicators included less developed social and communication skills as well as shyness, and fine and gross motor delays. The authors suggested that ASD might appear at different ages because environmental demands eventually exceed the child's capacity to deal with increasing demands, due to limitations caused by the disorder.

The approach used in the Bayley-4 ASD Checklist is simple: the more positive indicators observed during testing and verified by caregiver report, the greater the possibility of ASD that will need to be validated by a more detailed, ASD-specific evaluation. There is no cut score or critical number of items failed (although this would be good research question). One or two positive items most likely do not warrant further ASD workup or closer monitoring, unless there are other circumstances that would influence the examiner's decision to do so (ASD found in siblings, high degree of parental concern, advanced paternal age). Other physical and developmental problems (e.g., vision, hearing, motor, language) may mimic ASD symptoms and should also be considered. Examiners are advised to start at a level considered age-appropriate on the Bayley-4 ASD Checklist (determined by Bayley-4 start points); items below show that level could be explored via questioning the caregiver, if necessary. An item is considered "positive" if a score of "0" is obtained, *not* if the skill is emerging (score of "1"). Scores of 0 obtained on items above the child's age cannot be evaluated adequately.

Twenty-five Bayley-4 items are included in the checklist. An additional 10 items incidentally observed by the examiner that are atypical or unusual are also included. These items have been associated with ASD during previous Bayley testing and also have been indicated to be suggestive ASD by other investigators (e.g., Allison, Auyeung, & Baron-Cohen, 2012; Allison et al., 2008; Wetherby et al., 2004; Wiggins et al., 2014).

The 26 Bayley-4 ASD Checklist items are (Table A1. Bayley Technical Manual; Bayley & Aylward, 2019b):

CG (9)	recognizes caregiver (social/visual) reaction to caregiver (social/visual/learning) reacts to disappearance of caregiver (social) interacts with mirror image (social/interest in surroundings) pats table (imitation) stirs spoon (imitation) squeezes object (imitation) imitates two-step action (imitation) imaginary play (abstracting/imagination)
RC (4)	calms when spoken to (social [auditory]) responds to name (social/recognition) attends to play routine (maintains social interaction) understands pronouns (language [*two items*])
EC (12)	social smile (social interaction) social vocalizing/laughs (interaction) elicits attention/interaction (initiates social interaction) uses gestures (joint attention) jabbers expressively (communication) directs attention of adult to object (showing; joint attention) imitates word (verbal imitation) imitates play (imitation) combines gesture and words (higher order communication) uses pronouns (language) poses questions (initiates reciprocal communication) answers questions (responds-reciprocal communication)

Additional observational items (10) listed in the Appendix that raise concerns include:

- Child uses examiner's or caregiver's hands as a tool during testing (e.g., places adult's hand on desired object, versus asks for it).
- Atypical vocalizations (e.g., uses high-pitched voice, growls, screeches, consistently uses outside voice).
- Produces unusual syllable strings (e.g., uga-uga-uga; nkka-nkka-nkka)
- Prosody issues (e.g., no inflections; flat, robot-like manner of speaking; unusual voice quality)
- Echolalia/repetitive use of words; set use of phrases often out of context
- Repetitive or stereotyped use of Bayley test items (lines up blocks, pegs)
- Licks, smells, scratches test objects

- Unusual, often intense distress responses: excessively fearful, meltdowns when objects are removed, sudden changes in affect
- Does not transition easily through test tasks; not flexible
- Noted to stare blankly on multiple occasions during testing.

As stated previously, the Bayley-4 ASD Checklist does not yield a diagnosis per se. Rather, it tallies behaviors that may be indicative of ASD in a child who is being given a developmental assessment. Areas of function tapped on administered Bayley-4 items include imitation, social referencing, joint attention, and communication. Obviously, expressive communication contributes the most items. In addition, observational items delineate unusual or odd behaviors that are evident to an excessive degree and the combination of both groupings of items enables identification of patterns of behaviors that are concerning.

The Social-Emotional scale of the Bayley-4 also is very helpful in identifying children who manifest ASD symptoms. Poor self-regulation, inability to socially communicate, lack of emotional signals, or an inability to establish relationships are examples of behaviors that raise suspicion in the area of social communication. The sensory processing section of the Social-Emotional scale fits in the restricted/repetitive behavior criteria of DSM-5.

Caution must be exercised to ensure that the infant or toddler's performance on the ASD Checklist is not due to other specific causes such as a hearing impairment (the child might not respond to his or her name being called or does not imitate words), a language delay (does not combine gesture and words or use pronouns), or a motor problem (where the child might not be able to pat the table or stir with a spoon in imitation). Children with severe neurodevelopmental impairments have a greater likelihood of scoring positive on ASD Checklists in general. The high scores often are due to the degree of neurodevelopmental impairment, versus ASD per se.

Conversely, the presence of certain behaviors is contraindicative of the likelihood of ASD. These include:

- The child seeks interactions with others as evident during the testing situation and per parent report.
- The infant displays a wide range of affect, appropriate to the situation.
- The toddler manifests sustained, *meaningful* eye contact (not fleeting, does not look primarily at the examiner's or caregiver's mouth when he/she speaks)
- There is frequent imitation of the examiner and/or caregiver
- Verbalizations and gestures are used for communication

- The infant/toddler complies with the examiner's requests regarding test manipulatives. He or she does not get locked excessively into certain routines with test materials in comparison to others the same age and relinquishes them on request.
- There are no repetitive, restricted behaviors noted during testing or reported by caregiver.
- The infant or toddler initiates interactive games such as purposefully dropping a test item and laughing in anticipation of the examiner picking it up.

Finally, tying this into the neuro-environmental synthesis model outlined in Chapter 1, weaker interhemispheric connections in the inferior frontal gyrus and superior temporal gyrus—areas important in language production and comprehension—are found in children with ASD (Dinstein et al., 2011). This suggests problems with lateral versus vertical circuitry, which could be the result of epigenetic influences.

Clinicians may be interested to know that, with regard to genetics and epigenetic influences, ASD is now known to involve both rare, de novo copy number variants (deletions and duplications) and more common variants (Woodbury-Smith & Scherer, 2018). The possibility exists that a number of children have low penetrance mutations that predispose them to ASD, but do not develop the disorder unless there is a "second hit" such as maternal infection in-utero, exposure to toxicants, inflammation, or disruption in brain development due to prematurity—any of which then produces the clinical phenotype of ASD (Woodbury-Smith & Scherer, 2018). This finding also may explain the large degree of phenotypic variation in the disorder. This is an intriguing area of investigation and answers will become clearer in the future.

CHAPTER 9

Bayley-4 accommodations and modifications

Contents

When using standardized norm-referenced tests (SNRAs) with infants and toddlers who have specific disabilities, examiners often need to make adjustments to the testing procedures to circumvent the potential negative effects the disabilities may have on test performance. This is particularly true when evaluating an infant who has a visual impairment, a neuromotor disorder, or a hearing impairment.

The goal of assessment is to obtain an accurate estimate of a child's abilities, while still maintaining the validity and integrity of the standardized administration and scoring. This is especially important when testing children with specific impairments, because they will be compared to standardized test norms from peers without disabilities. In a child with a sensory or motor disability, adaptations to item presentation, materials, timing, or response format may be necessary to determine strengths and weaknesses. Qualitative information regarding which adaptations seem to work over the course of the evaluation is also important in subsequent development of the child's intervention programming.

Accommodations versus modifications

The terms, *accommodations* and *modifications*, are often used interchangeably to describe adaptations to developmental testing, but these terms differ significantly. Accommodations are defined as acceptable or permissible changes in

Bayley 4 Clinical Use and Interpretation
https://doi.org/10.1016/B978-0-12-817754-9.00009-X

materials or procedures used during testing (Thurlow, Elliott, & Ysseldyke, 2003). The purposes of accommodations in children with disabilities are to increase the validity of inferences made from their test scores and identify capabilities that might be obscured by their disability under standardized administration conditions. Moreover, accommodations circumvent the potential negative impact of a disability and allow demonstration of the child's knowledge. Therefore, performance regarding the developmental construct under consideration, versus interfering testing issues, is actually measured.

Assessment of children with major disabilities is difficult and adaptations typically are necessary. Accommodations can promote accurate measurement of a specific construct and allow comparison across examinees, regardless of the presence of a disability. However, because accommodations are variations in the way a test is presented, these should not be used simply to improve test scores. If accommodations do not change the standardized test stimuli or procedures, scoring will not be affected and normative scores can be used for comparative purposes. If accommodations are instituted, these should be specified.

In contrast, a modification is a change in the *content* of the test itself. It is considered to be a change in the actual construct being measured, rather than an alteration in the administration format. Modifications preclude comparison to the normative test data, and therefore, should be avoided because the validity of the data is questionable.

The type, severity, and how the disability is manifest will help determine and guide the administration and adaptations of the test. Zimmerman, Steiner, and Pond (2002) caution that when standardized procedures are modified, normative scores should *not* be reported.

Accommodations for Bayley-4 cognitive, language, and motor scales

The Bayley-4 includes features such as using adaptive equipment for positioning, testing with the child facing the examiner while seated on the caregiver's lap, and allowance for a variety of individualized response types (see Appendix C in Bayley-4 Administration Manual; Bayley & Aylward, 2019a). Accommodations for the Bayley-4 allow for minor adjustments in the placement of materials (e.g., moving an item closer to a child with a visual impairment; repeating instructions accompanied with gestures for a child with compromised hearing). In addition, the Bayley-4 has other features that facilitate its use with children who have disabilities:

- Items have simplified directions when possible.
- The amount of language involved in directions is decreased for nonlanguage tasks.
- Directions are less scripted or rigid and contain more flexibility.
- Caregiver report can be utilized on items.
- Many items are scored by observation, allowing assessment of spontaneous, specific behaviors and how the child adapts when displaying these behaviors.

Several items allow provision of naturalistic or "authentic" directional cues (e.g., gestures) as well as verbal instructions to allow for a more flexible presentation format. For example, in the "place the block in the cup" item, the examiner tells the child to put the block in the cup accompanied by a gesture of pointing from the block to the cup. This can be done several times. Demonstration of the form board item with both verbal instructions and pointing is another example.

Many items allow for approximations of responses which indicate an understanding of the construct being measured and basic skills but not mastery. For example, the polytomous 2, 1, 0, scoring scheme also allows for credit when the child's disability interferes with a two-point response to a task, but there is evidence of an emerging skill (earning a one-point response). This should be mentioned in any subsequent narrative or test report.

The Bayley-4 also provides acceptable, graded levels of support when needed during the administration of an item. When assessing the infant's ability to manipulate blocks, Level I support involves the examiner placing blocks one at a time on the table. Level II support is holding the block in front of the child, while Level III support involves actually placing the block in the child's hand. Noteworthy is the fact that this behavior will not invalidate the items. Nonetheless, the type of supports used should also be mentioned in the examiner's report.

An acceptable strategy for obtaining both quantitative and qualitative information starts with standardized administration; if the child cannot complete an item successfully, administration can be adjusted incrementally. Other testing strategies may include providing a variety of cues and prompts and adjustments regarding feedback and reinforcement of the child's responses (i.e., praise, giving "high fives," etc.).

Each child with a disability is unique and there is no specific accommodation that is appropriate for all children. General approaches to infants and toddlers with various disabilities are outlined below.

The child with visual impairment

Visual impairments are conditions in which a child's visual abilities, even with maximum correction, are insufficient to allow "normal" visually mediated daily functions. These impairments also include significantly decreased visual acuity or restrictions in visual field. Severity of visual impairment in infants and young children is often difficult to determine accurately. A considerable number of infants and toddlers diagnosed with a visual impairment also have co-occurring disabilities, most notably intellectual disability or cerebral palsy (Vohr et al., 2012).

Children referred for Bayley-4 assessments may have undiagnosed visual impairments. Potential indicators of visual impairment include:

- Infant does not turn his or her head toward a light; does not track a small light while in a semidarkened room
- The infant shows minimal interest in visual stimuli or does not track high contrast stimuli
- The infant displays abnormal eye movements or positioning (e.g., nystagmus, strabismus (esotropia or exotropia))
- Objects are brought close to the face or the child brings his or her face close to table in order to view test items
- Oversensitivity to light often evident by squinting or irritability

To accommodate children with visual impairment, the following techniques may be employed:

- Position test items where the child can best see them. Optimum placement may vary, depending on the child and various approaches should be tried. Some children may require magnifying aids.
- Avoid glare on the table or test materials. Adjust lighting accordingly.
- Extra time should be allowed for the child to scan visual stimuli.
- If the child wears glasses, these should also be employed during testing sessions.
- Increase the visibility of test materials by enhancing contrast of the table surface. Use a large piece of paper or placemat with contrasting color.
- Because visual impairment can affect upper extremity function, allow the child to hold and manipulate items, or place them into his or her hands.

If a child requires modifications of materials and methods due to accommodations being ineffective, normative data should not be used for comparative purposes. Examples of such modifications include use of different materials from home such as spinners, vibrating toys, and toys with augmented sensory stimuli. These modifications, however, do provide qualitative, descriptive data and this information is highly useful.

The child with hearing impairment

Hearing impairment is another low-incidence disability that is on a continuum from severe (deaf) to mild (hard of hearing). Hearing impairment significantly affects both expressive and receptive language and has an impact on cognitive and social development as well (Vohr et al., 2012). The degree of hearing loss, the child's age at which the loss occurred, the age at which the loss was identified, and the interventions used to address the loss are mitigating factors.

Risk factors associated with hearing impairment in young infants (Joint Committee on Infant Hearing, 2000) include:

- Family history of hearing loss;
- Maternal infection during pregnancy such as rubella, syphilis, toxoplasmosis, herpes, or cytomegalovirus (CMV);
- Craniofacial anomalies;
- History of bacterial meningitis;
- Hyperbilirubinemia, kernicterus;
- Findings associated with a genetic syndrome whose phenotype includes sensorineural and/or conductive hearing loss;
- Birth weight less than 1500 g (VLBW); gestational age <32 weeks;
- Exposure to ototoxic medications;
- Significant hypoxic ischemic encephalopathy (HIE).

Some children pass an early hearing screening (e.g., in the nursery), but subsequently are found to have hearing issues. Older infants and toddlers should receive an audiologic evaluation if any of the following risk factors are reported:

- Caregiver concerns about hearing, or delay in speech or language;
- Inconsistent responsiveness to sounds or voices;
- Head trauma;
- Recurrent or persistent otitis media with effusion;
- Eustachian tube dysfunction;
- Childhood infectious diseases known to be associated with hearing loss;
- Child speaks in an excessively loud manner or only says first syllable of words;
- Child cannot discriminate high frequency consonants such as "f," "th," or "sh."

There is great variability in both receptive and expressive communication skills in children with hearing loss. However, there is a relationship between the degree of hearing loss and the degree of impairment in language skills.

Testing guidelines and accommodations for children with hearing impairment include:

- Any amplification system routinely used by the child should be employed in the Bayley-4 administration.
- Ambient noise should be minimized (e.g., blowers, fans, air conditioners, loud hallway conversations).
- If the examiner is uncertain as to what the child said, this should be verified with the caregiver as to what the child was trying to convey. Understanding the child typically improves with more exposure.
- If a sign translator participates in testing, he or she should sit beside or slightly behind the examiner in full view of the child.

Caution should be exercised when parents, other adult relatives, or a child's siblings are used as interpreters. As a general rule, use of these individuals for this role is not recommended.

The child with motor impairment

Accommodation strategies are necessary to negate effects of motor problems on the child's test performance (in both motor and cognitive tasks). Motor involvement is particularly disruptive in the young child because motor and cognitive functions are heavily interrelated in many of the test tasks at this age. Assessment becomes easier when cognitive and motor functions diverge with advancing age. Alternate modes of response may be considered such as eye gaze, blinking, or vocalizing when the examiner points to the item choice the child wants to select (the latter arguably being considered a modification by some).

Materials may need to be presented very close to a child who has decreased arm mobility or limited reaching ability. Moving the item closer, stabilizing a body part, or stabilizing the materials with Velcro or tape are acceptable accommodations.

Good clinical skills are needed to recognize the child's subtle behavioral changes during testing that may include: (1) facial brightening and gestures; (2) changes in posture or tone such as body stiffening; (3) changes in activity level; (4) alterations in eye gaze or changes in facial expression (smiling or frowning); or (5) becoming relaxed and quiet.

Accommodations described previously with regard to visual or hearing impairments are also appropriate for children with motor impairments.

There is a Dutch Bayley-III low motor/vision test which includes adaptations for low motor abilities and low vision (Visser, Ruiter, van der Meulen, Ruijssenaars, & Timmerman, 2014). These adaptations include test material accommodations (larger manipulatives—making them easier to handle and to see), instructional accommodations (allows "eye-pointing" instead of finger pointing, support of child's elbow by the examiner), and procedural accommodations (elimination of time limits). Accommodations were found to not increase the scores of typically developing control children, but did improve scores in 56% of impaired children on the Cognitive scale. However, if the impairment was severe, accommodations did not prove to be helpful (Visser, Ruiter, van der Meulen, Ruijssenaars, & Timmerman, 2013). Although potentially useful for the Bayley-4 in the future, the number of children who have been involved in these studies has been limited and more data are necessary.

"Tricks of the trade"

Unfortunately, examiners frequently encounter a child who is reluctant to cooperate unless the testing is on his or her terms, is shy, or is slow-to-warm-up. Subtle, serendipitous clues of developmental problems during testing may occur and could be missed if the examiner was not looking for them. Unlike Adaptive functioning where the behavior of interest must be *routinely demonstrated* and the capacity to perform the elicited task is not of primary importance, in evaluation of cognitive, language, and motor skills, the *capacity* to clearly perform the task is of interest. There are accommodations for these less-than-cooperative types which can be utilized without actually modifying the test item to the point that it is no longer valid.

As a general rule, when testing a child who is anxious, shy, or flat out oppositional, examiners should encourage caregiver participation as much as possible. For example, rather than giving the child a block, have the caregiver do so. Prior to administration of an item, the caregiver should be cautioned to not: (a) be too directive, (b) actually do the task for the child, or (c) give feedback or cues that would facilitate a higher score (e.g., telling the child "no, try again" or "are you sure that's where the circle goes?"). Humor, good-natured chiding and modeling by the examiner can usually suffice in stopping the interfering caregiver behavior. A second general suggestion is to make the testing fun for the child and caretaker: liberal use of praise, "high fives," applause, and "good job" help in that regard. If the caregiver is at ease, the child will be as well. If both are at ease, there is a good chance the examiner will also be equally relaxed and everyone will be in good ease nirvana. At the outset, the caregiver should be cautioned not to "ask" the child to do a task, but rather tell him or her to do it in a gently declarative fashion. The question, "Can you stack these blocks for me?," provides an excellent opening for a resounding "NO!" from the child—a response not to be swayed by "pretty please?." Over the years, I have seen many a well-intentioned pediatrics resident on the developmental/behavioral rotation break down into a pleading mess after receiving the big "NO!" in front of observers, be unable to persuade the child to cooperate any further, and have the session come to an abrupt termination—a matter-of-fact, "Okay let's stack the blocks" works much better.

A frequent behavior that interferes with testing of infants <12 months of age is a prominent mouthing schema. Basically, the infant is processing the environment by oral exploration. Anything small enough to go into the mouth, will (even larger objects will be sampled in this manner). If a pacifier doesn't alleviate the situation, examiners will have to try their best to quickly retrieve the test items before they get to the infant's mouth. Caregivers can be very helpful in that regard.

Although not necessarily reflected in the score of a test item, *how* the infant or toddler approaches or accomplishes a task should be noted. An example is found with the blue board series. Some toddlers will use a trial-and-error approach with each round or square form, while others will look at the form and immediately put it in the proper hole. The latter behavior reflects a qualitatively different approach which is suggestive of a higher order understanding of the concept and more advanced working memory skills.

In receptive and expressive communication tasks, the examiner is sometimes faced with idiosyncratic names used in the infant's household which, nonetheless, reflect an understanding of the picture or object. The toddler might call a cup "coffee" or "tea," or a picture of a dog by the family dog's name. These responses are indicative of an understanding of the word or concept and are often acceptable. When social commands are employed, the caregiver or examiner should not use gestures (e.g., wave "bye-bye"). Although gestures are definitely a form of communication, in this case we are specifically assessing verbal comprehension.

If the toddler refuses to point to pictures named by the examiner, this can be circumvented by giving the child a block and asking him or her to place it on the picture that is being named. As in the case of a child with motor impairment, if the toddler refuses to point to the picture or place a block, but unambiguously looks at the picture named, this again reflects understanding. The child should also be asked to point to their own body parts first; if this is not successful, then he or she can be requested to point to the caregiver's body parts.

As a general rule, the examiner should be familiar with the items in the age range of the child who is being tested, including pathognomonic indicators or "red flags" that often occur at that age (Chapter 10).

Finally, when administering early gross motor tasks, it is helpful to have the caregiver place the infant on the examination table or mat for items such as pull-to-sit, crawling, head control when prone, or similar items. Many infants become frightened when this is done by a stranger.

CHAPTER 10

Indicators of abnormality (red flags)

Contents

Administration of the Bayley-4 items provides the opportunity to detect pathognomonic indicators over the course of the evaluation session. These indicators are "red flags," suggestive of underlying developmental problems. Because the incidence of these indicators is low even in clinical populations, most were not formally included in the Bayley-4 item set. Nonetheless, as part of the overall clinical evaluation, examiners should note when these behaviors are observed, as these typically are not the result of maturational lags or delays, but are due to deficits or deviance in development or neurological impairment (Accardo, Accardo, & Capute, 2008; Aylward, 1997).

It must be emphasized that *patterns* of dysfunction are more concerning than is an *individual* "abnormal" sign. The *functional impact* or significance of an abnormal or questionable finding is also important, namely, how does the finding affect the child's development? For example, tightness of the lower extremities in a 14-month-old child is less concerning if he or she is able to walk unassisted (suggesting minimal functional impact) than if the toddler was unable to ambulate at all because she stands on her tiptoes constantly or walks in an unstable, awkward manner, indicating that increased tone was having a negative effect on development of this skill.

Bayley 4 Clinical Use and Interpretation
https://doi.org/10.1016/B978-0-12-817754-9.00010-6

Delay, dissociation, and deviance

The concepts of *delay*, *dissociation*, and *deviance* are important in the evaluation of developmental problems (Accardo et al., 2008). A *delay* occurs when an infant does not reach developmental milestones or master skills at the expected age, despite allowing for the relatively broad variation inherent in "normality." The lag could occur in one or more areas of function and is not abnormal per se because it is expected that the toddler will "catch up" at some point; however, the term cannot be used indefinitely. Bayley-4 items that are scored with a "1" (emerging) may be associated with delays. A *dissociation* refers to a significant difference in the evolving rates of two developmental domains such as a major discrepancy between receptive and expressive language abilities or verbal and visual processing skills. A dissociation also occurs if two typically related or linked developmental acquisitions do not occur together such as being able to crawl but not sit unsupported. A dissociation is not necessarily abnormal in and of itself, but there is an increased possibility that it might be indicative of later abnormality. *Deviance* is an atypical or nonsequential unevenness in the appearance of milestones or an atypical developmental indicator that is abnormal at any age (e.g., cortical thumbing, extreme hypertonicity of the lower extremities, nystagmus, lack of any verbalizations) (Accardo et al., 2008). Many of these indicators warrant a Bayley-4 score of "0."

Vision/motor/tone indicators

Visual

Whenever Bayley-4 visual items are administered (e.g., visually follows ring, follows pencil, or looks at pellet), examiners should monitor deviations in the infant's gaze, aberrant eye positioning, or uncoordinated eye movements. The "*setting sun sign*" is a downward conjugate deviation of gaze accompanied by retraction of the upper eyelid, lowering of the globe, and exposed sclera over the top rim of the iris (hence the setting sun analogy). This aberrant positioning may be indicative of increased intracranial compression or pressure. *Nystagmus* is indicated by involuntary, rhythmical, conjugate oscillatory (side-to-side) movements that can be slow (pendular) or jerky. Nystagmus may be observed when the child is visually tracking, or it could be present constantly (as in the case of cortical blindness). This problem may be due to a variety of ophthalmological and neurological conditions involving the central nervous system (CNS), eye, or inner ear. *Strabismus* is a condition in which the eyes are not maintained parallel, with one or both eyes deviating inward (*esotropia*) or outward (*exotropia*) (Aylward, 1997; Baird & Gordon, 1983). This may be surgically corrected or treated with eye patching.

Neurological signs/tone

Several neurological signs have prognostic significance in infancy (Hamer & Hadders-Algra, 2016). In early infancy (during the first several months), absence of *a Moro response* or absence of *a plantar grasp reflex* (GM 19 on the Bayley-4) is predictive of later neuromotor problems such as cerebral palsy (CP). After early infancy, persistence of the Moro (> 4 months of age), *the asymmetric tonic neck response* (> 5 months; GM 12), and absence of or asymmetry in the *forwards parachute response* (> 9 months; GM 14) may be indicative of CP or other motor deficits. Head lag in *the pull-to-sit maneuver* (GM 21) and "slip-through" in the *vertical suspension test* (infant is lifted straight up with the examiner's hands placed under the child's armpits (axillae) but shoulder tone is weak) are significant red flags of hypotonicity throughout infancy (Hamer & Hadders-Algra, 2016).

With regard to muscle tone, bilateral use of the upper and lower extremities and comparable tone and movement on both sides of the body should be present. *Hypotonia* (decreased muscle tone) is one of the most frequent pathognomonic indicators, being caused by CNS, metabolic, or neuromuscular disorders. Full-term infants with hypoxic ischemic encephalopathy often display decreased tone (Douglas-Escobar & Weiss, 2015). This can be observed in Bayley-4 head control items (e.g., rights head, pulls to sit, head control when sitting; e.g., GM 8, 21) as well as in administration of other gross motor items. If a child cannot sit without support by 7–8 months, this is a significant concern.

Conversely, many infants born preterm (33%–50%, depending on the gestational age) show *hypertonia* (increased tone) and a constellation of factors often termed "*transient dystonia of prematurity*" (de Vries & de Groot, 2002). This condition is characterized by increased tone of the lower extremities, tight heel cords, brisk patellar tendon reflexes, back and neck arching, and increased axial (truncal) tone. Hypertonia is highest at 3–4 months and decreases thereafter, improving in the majority of infants by 12 months (seen in Bayley-4 items such as pulls-to-sit, parachute reactions, rolls from back to stomach; GM 9, 14, 21, 23). Although there is general improvement in tone over the first 18–24 months, if the infant shows early tone abnormalities, there is increased risk of emergence of later, high prevalence/low severity dysfunctions (e.g., ADHD, learning disabilities, executive dysfunction, visual-motor integration difficulties, low average to borderline IQ) (Aylward, 2005).

The "scarf sign" allows assessment of the shoulder girdle tone in infants. The child is placed in a supine position and the arm is gently pulled to the opposite shoulder until resistance occurs. The elbow position in relation to the midline is evaluated. With low tone, the elbow crosses the midline to the opposite (contralateral) midpoint of the clavicle (collar bone). High tone is suspected if the elbow does not cross the ipsilateral (same side) midpoint of the clavicle (Noritz, Murphy, and Neuromotor Screening Expert Panel, 2013).

Similarly, tone of the lower extremities can be assessed via the "popliteal angle." The infant again is placed supine, the hip is flexed 90 degrees from the table, and the leg is slowly extended. If the infant is hypertonic, the angle between the lower leg and vertical is < 6 degrees; with high tone, it is ≥ 50 degrees (Noritz, Murphy, & Neuromotor Screening Expert Panel, 2013).

Milestones

Some major gross motor milestones and their age ranges include pulls to standing by 9–12 months, cruises around furniture 11–14 months, walks 9–17 months, runs 15–20 months, and jumps off the floor with both feet leaving the surface, 24–34 months (these ages are in the average to the high end of normal range). These milestones are found on the Bayley-4. With regard to protective reactions such as the downwards or forwards parachute maneuvers, scissoring of the legs with feet pointed down in the downwards parachute (i.e., crossing one over the other) is often indicative of spasticity and is usually accompanied by increased tone of the legs and brisk patellar reflexes. Asymmetry in arm extension in the forward parachute maneuver is suggestive of possible hemiplegia. Again, these items are observable during administration of the Bayley-4.

With respect to fine motor functions, lack of midline behaviors by 6-months, an inability to pick up a second block while retaining the first, transfer a block or ring, or bang objects, as well as poor distal flexibility seen in the wrist rotation item (e.g., FM 10, 16) or having a strongly established hand preference prior to 24–36 months should be considered red flags—it is particularly concerning if the infant displays an obvious hand preference prior to 12 months of age. Poor motor modulation, evident in tasks involving reaching, grasping, or releasing objects (reaches/obtains objects, releasing blocks in a cup, block stacking series), is also a concern. With regard to several early fine motor milestones (mean age to upper end of normal), hands should not be fisted by 3–4 months (FM 8), transfer should occur by 5–7 months, and a neat pincer grasp should be present by 9–10 months (FM 19). By 12 months, the infant should feed himself or herself finger foods (FM 17).

Handedness may also be indicative of possible neuromotor problems. For example, a twofold increase in left and/or nonright handedness (ambiguous or mixed-handedness) is found in preterm infants, the rate being 22% versus 12% in controls (Domellof, Johansson, & Ronnqvist, 2011). It is hypothesized that this difference is due to some type of subtle brain insult or disruption of normal brain developmental sequences. Moreover, an increased frequency of mixed-handedness (not specifically left-handedness) has been reported in children with neurodevelopmental disorders (Domellof, Ronnqvist, Titram, Esseily, & Fagard, 2009). That is not to say, however, that left-handedness is abnormal.

Cerebral palsy

The concept of *cerebral palsy* (CP) deserves discussion. This is a broadly defined disorder and may be manifest in abnormalities of tone, movement, or posture. Sometimes CP is only evident when a toddler is engaged in activities that involve motor coordination or regulation of muscle tone which place increased demands on the child making these abnormalities more evident. Indicators may surface as an inability to restrict movements to an intended pattern or location (e.g., overshooting), tremors, or excessive motor overflow (one hand mimicking the movements of another).

Historically, the diagnosis of CP is made between 12 and 24 months (Novak, Hines, Goldsmith, & Barclay, 2012; Novak, Spirit Jones, & Morgan, 2017), although more recently some investigators suggest it can be made by 6 months. Earlier age of diagnosis most likely depends on the severity of CP, with more severe cases becoming apparent earlier. Moreover, although CP is due to a static injury to the brain, the outward manifestations may change over time. Many infants first display hypotonia at 6–12 weeks of age, followed by a dystonic stage (poor quality of movement, diffuse increase in tone) and then spasticity becomes more evident at 8–9 months. The toddler will often become obviously spastic by 24 months. *Spastic diplegia* (symmetric hypertonicity of the lower extremities) is found mostly in those born preterm and spastic hemiplegia (hypertonicity on one side of the body with arm more involved than the leg) can be detected in infancy; *quadriplegic cerebral palsy* (abnormal tone involving all four extremities as well as the head and trunk) is often detected by 5 months. As a general rule, preterm infants tend to display hypertonicity; hypotonicity is more frequently found in at-risk full-terms. Bayley-4 FM and GM items, such as keeping hands open, palmar grasp reflex, grasping ring (FM 5, 8, 9), or displaying coordinated running (GM 42), provide opportunities to observe these potential red flags. With older children, examiners should pay particular attention to any gait problems such as dragging a leg, running in an awkward, clumsy manner, being unable to quickly stop when running, unusual posturing of the arms or hands when walking or running, or similar behaviors.

Several other early motor/tone indicators are considered to be important indicators of increased risk for later problems: *neck extensor hypertonia* (seen in pull to sit), *truncal tone hypertonicity* (increased axial (core) tone resulting in difficulty with sitting items, the infant typically pushing backwards), *poor visual following* (head tracking items), and an *asymmetric tonic neck posturing that persists* past 5–6 months (Bayley-4 ATNR item). *Asymmetric postures, hypo- or hyperkinesis* (underactivity/overactivity), are also of concern. Symmetry in motor movements and tone should be evident.

Minor Neurological Dysfunction (MND) is used to describe children of 18 months and older who do not have CP, but still have some neurological impairment. Often this is not diagnosed until 4 years of age (Hutchon, 2018). MND is not a formal neurologic diagnosis, but is a description of the child's neurological profile which includes: difficulties with posture, muscle tone regulation, balance, mildly abnormal reflexes, and problematic coordination (Brostrom, Vollmer, Bolk, Eklof, & Aden, 2018). Functionally, these children have problems with manual dexterity, aiming, balance, and catching. A greater incidence of later ADHD is associated with MND (Brostrom et al., 2018). MND can be classified as simple or complex, depending on the number of domains that are dysfunctional. Simple MND is either genetic or due to stress in early postnatal life which affects the monoaminergic system (e.g., dopamine, norepinephrine); complex MND is due to dysfunctional cortico-striatal-thalmo-cortical circuits (also involved in cognitive and behavioral development) (Hadders-Algra, 2002). MND symptoms are apparent on the Bayley-4 after age 2 years of age.

Clusters of abnormalities, motor or otherwise, are much more reliable in the prediction of later dysfunction than are isolated signs. The predictive power of abnormal findings and the amount of concern increase corresponding to an increase in the number of these findings. The *functional significance* of an abnormal finding is critical. For example, if the child shows a mild increase in tone, but is able to crawl with relatively good coordination or cruise around furniture and lower himself fairly smoothly to the floor, then the impact of the increased tone is minimal. Similarly, examiners should be cautious using average ages as a gauge for when a developmental milestone should occur. By virtue of being average, ½ of the children will fall above that age of skill acquisition and many still might be within normal limits; it has been argued that the 75th or 90th percentiles should be used for milestones instead.

Social interaction and communication

The following behaviors that can be observed during the Bayley-4 administration raise concerns in this area of development and often are associated with *autism spectrum disorders* (ASD). See ASD Indicators checklist (Chapter 8; Appendix A of Bayley-4 Technical Manual) as well.

- Does not smile or interact with caregiver by 6 months
- Inappropriate or no eye contact; does not hold attention, not aware of surroundings (e.g., assess with Bayley-4 items: reaction to caregiver, responds to surroundings, social smile, solicits attention/interaction)
- Disinterest in materials or objects (reaches/obtains objects, obtains ring on Bayley-4)
- Does not engage in social routines (items: responds to request for social routines, attends to play routine). No turn-taking or participation in games such as peek-a-boo.
- Does not display babbling that mimics actual talking in terms of cadence, sounds, etc. by 12 months
- No pretend play (relational play, representational play)
- Failure to show gestural or verbal communication (Bayley-4 items use gestures, combines gestures and words)
- Odd rhythm, cadence, or prosody to language (expressive communication items); poor language pragmatics (turn-taking in conversation)
- Lacks interest in playing or interacting with others by 18 months.
- Perseverative behaviors: has to have things done in a certain way or objects placed in a certain order, "locks onto" certain test materials, uses test materials in own venue (observation of performance on cognitive, and communication items).
- Overreactivity/underreactivity to sensory stimuli, avoids physical contact (calms when picked up), overreacts to sounds (reacts to sounds in environment, discriminates sounds, plays with paper). The Social-emotional sensory scale is highly useful in evaluating these sensory issues.

Attention/executive function

Executive function early on is more general, versus having more discrete, specific functions. Nonetheless, early indicators of executive dysfunction are found in the Bayley-4. These include:

- Very short attention span for age; cannot sustain attention for more than a few seconds, does not persevere on tasks (e.g., Bayley-4 items: shifts attention, explores object, anticipatory gaze, searches for missing objects, places pellets in bottle)
- Child acts in an overly impulsive manner for age, frequently not waiting for instructions, grabbing manipulatives, not staying seated for any sustained period of time, always moving. Validity of such behavior should be ascertained by caregiver report.
- Does not seem aware of surroundings.

Red flags can be found with regard to motor, cognitive, language, social, and/or adaptive function. Examiners using the Bayley-4 are advised to note these indicators, but should not venture a diagnosis based on them, particularly if the findings are isolated. Development of these skills will differentiate clinicians from technicians. These red flags should be included in the testing report and transmitted to the child's primary care physician for referral for more specific evaluation(s) by neurology, physical therapy, occupational therapy, or speech/language specialists.

Summary

In summary, the sequence or pattern of development is remarkably consistent.

However, the rate at which developmental skills are mastered is highly variable. Moreover, some milestones are more consistent than others. Nonetheless, there are certain findings that are particularly worrisome:

- Any loss of a previously acquired skill
- Frequent "limit ages" for developmental acquisitions are noted. More specifically, skills typically achieved at ages that are close to two standard deviations from the mean (this falling in the bottom 3%)
- Caregivers' concerns regarding the child's vision or hearing
- No independent walking by 18 months
- No reaching behaviors by 6 months
- Emotional dysregulation

A unique approach: Optimality

A different way of viewing critical items on the Bayley-4 warrants brief mention. The method involves identification of test items and behaviors which potentially are prognostic indicators of later *positive*, versus *negative* outcome. This is termed the *optimality approach* and was used initially with antenatal and perinatal risk scales (in contrast to complications scales). This framework subsequently was applied to neurologic findings (Haataja et al., 1999; Prechtl, 1980) and was incorporated into other tests, including the Bayley Infant Neurodevelopmental Screener (Aylward, 1995). These tests included a tally of optimal responses and optimality was based on distribution of scores that are associated with more positive outcomes. With the Bayley-4, more complex items that involve higher order processing were selected to produce an informal optimality index. Essentially, a "normal" (optimal) finding (a score of 2) on an item that is complex is considered to have a higher predictive value for later, age-appropriate functioning than does an "abnormal" response (score of 0) being predictive of later abnormal functioning. Furthermore, the association with positive outcome is strengthened with increasing numbers of these optimal responses. The major premise is that emphasis should be placed on the tasks the child *can* do successfully and which require complex processing. Because these tasks involve integrated neural networks, optimality is more than a simple "the glass is half full" versus "the glass is half empty" approach to viewing development.

If the child possesses the capacity to successfully perform more complex tasks, there is evidence that brain connectivity is intact. Items and behaviors that involve learning, aspects of executive function, problem solving, information processing, planning, flexibility in applying skills to new situations, and imagination are processes found in cognitive tasks which are suggestive of optimality (Chapter 3). Examples of specific Bayley-4 *cognitive items* that involve more complex processing and the functions that are tapped are listed below. This list is not intended to be exhaustive and these skills are more apparent at older ages.

There are numerous reasons for a child to not successfully complete a test task (e.g., developmental delay, resistance, a specific deficit in a certain area). Based on the neuro-environmental synthesis model, cognition necessary to successfully complete a complex task is dependent on the orchestrated information flow between neurons across extended white matter pathways. These pathways involve both local and long-distance interconnections

Item (CG #; name)	Construct
8: shifts attention	***Attention/Habituation***
9, 10, 11: Habituates	"
12: responds to surroundings	"
41: listens to story	"
20: pats table	***Imitation/learning***
29: stirs spoon	"
24: anticipatory gaze	"
28, 32, 37: searches for missing objects	***Object permanency***
34: removes pellet	***Problem solving***
51: rotated pink board	"
39, 44, 50, 59: play items	***Imagination/creativity***
56: spatial memory-3 cards	***Working memory***
60: recalls names	"
64: repeats words	"
76: spatial memory-6 cards	"
80: number sequences	"
62: groups-color	***Conceptualization***
63: groups-size	"
66: matches size	"
68: simple pattern	"
69: sorts pegs-color	"
81: completes pattern	"

(Chapter 1), and the connectivity patterns determine advances in developmental function.

Therefore, just as it is necessary to describe a toddler's areas of difficulty and "red flag" indicators, it is important to identify items that involve integrative processing that the child successfully completes. Presence of such skills supports a more optimistic prognosis. Although there currently are no optimality scales or scores per se for the Bayley-4, examiners may benefit from culling a performance profile from the above listing of the more complex test tasks. This would be an excellent area for future research.

CHAPTER 11

Clinical group studies

Contents

The Bayley-4 normative sample scores were compared to specific clinical groups in order to establish clinical validity (Bayley & Aylward, 2019b). The discriminative ability of the Bayley-4 is established by comparing infants and toddlers with specific diagnoses that place them at risk for developmental problems to matched controls. These comparisons are also helpful for clinicians who work with special populations. Clinical groups in these validity comparisons include infants and toddlers with Down Syndrome (DS), Motor Impairment (mild to moderate CP or Developmental Coordination Disorder), Autism Spectrum Disorders (ASD), Language Delay/Developmental Language Disorder (LD/SLI), Prematurity (those born Very/Extremely premature (V/EPT; <32 weeks); those born Moderately/Late premature (M/LPT; 32–36 weeks)), children with prenatal exposure to toxicants (alcohol, drugs: PDAE), and those with documented developmental delay (DD).

A description of the condition and results of matched comparisons for each of these at-risk groups follow.

Children with down syndrome

Down syndrome is probably the most common genetic cause of mild to moderate intellectual disability. Approximately 6000 babies are born with this *established risk* each year (1 in 700 live births; Parker et al., 2010).

Bayley 4 Clinical Use and Interpretation
https://doi.org/10.1016/B978-0-12-817754-9.00011-8

The likelihood of DS increases from 1 in 1300 at maternal age 25 to 1 in 55 by age 42. However, due to higher fertility rates in younger women, 80% of children with DS are born to women younger than 35 years of age. Approximately 95% of children with DS have Trisomy 21, 3% have translocation DS, and 2% have Mosaic Down syndrome. Down syndrome is associated with mild to moderate intellectual disability, characteristic facial features, and other physical issues (e.g., hearing loss, sleep apnea, ear infections, cardiac problems, and thyroid disease). IQ scores for children with DS are reported to typically be in the 50–60 range (although there is variability). Developmental delay and hypotonia are early characteristics. The highest developmental scores in children with Down Syndrome are obtained during infancy, with a progressive decline as the child ages (Dykens, Hodapp, & Evans, 1994). Therefore, scores of children with DS on the Bayley-4 can be expected to be higher the younger the child is when tested.

With regard to a cognitive phenotype, in addition to mild to moderate intellectual disability, weaknesses in expressive language, syntactic processing, and verbal working memory are frequently found. A developmental language delay is virtually always present, with expressive functions being more impaired than receptive skills (Moldavsky, Lev, & Lerman-Sagie, 2001). This profile of deficits may be the result of a failure to develop automatic processing in speech perception and production, and the language deficit partially explains the decline in overall scores over time. Visuospatial memory is not as impaired.

The Bayley-4 was administered to 54 children with DS, ranging in age from 2 to 42 months. The mean subtest and composite scores for the Down syndrome group were ≥2 standard deviations lower than the matched control group. Both the Language Composite (68) and Motor composite scores (71) were well below same age peers without Down syndrome, as was the Cognitive score that fell at the 2nd percentile. The effect sizes for all mean score differences were large. More information regarding scores can be found in the Bayley-4 Technical manual (Bayley & Aylward, 2019b).

Children with motor impairment

Cerebral palsy

Cerebral palsy is a clinical syndrome characterized by nonprogressive brain disturbance which affects muscle tone, posture, or movement and evolves within the first years of life (Blair, 2010). The incidence of cerebral palsy (CP) in the general population is 1 in 500 live births and this figure increases in children exposed to asphyxia, extreme prematurity, or other nonoptimal pre- and perinatal events (Novak, Spirit Jones, & Morgan, 2017; Reid, Carlin, & Reddihough, 2011). The diagnosis is made between 12 and 24 months, although some investigators suggest it can be made as early as 6 months in as much as 43% of cases (Novak et al., 2017). Fifty to sixty percent of young children with CP fall into the mild range of intellectual disability. The greater the severity of CP, the greater the likelihood of a lower level of intellectual function (Adams-Chapman et al., 2018). In high-risk preterm populations, there has been a shift from severe toward more mild degrees of motor impairment in CP (Adams-Chapman et al., 2018). Children with CP tend to have higher fine motor scores compared to their gross motor functioning. This incongruence between fine and gross motor function in children with CP underscores the need to review both motor subscales of the Bayley-4 and the motor composite score (Adams-Chapman et al., 2018). In preterm infants, the prevalence of CP increases with IVH severity and is found in 19% and 50% of those with grades III and IV IVH, respectively (Christian et al., 2016).

If the degree of CP is severe, information gleaned by comparison to a matched normative sample would be limited. Therefore, only children with mild to moderate CP were included in the clinical sample. The severity was verified when possible by the Gross Motor Functional Classification System scores of I–II (mild) or III (moderate) (GMFCS; Palisano, Rosenbaum, Bartlett, & Livingston, 2008; Palisano et al., 1997).

Developmental coordination disorders

Developmental Coordination Disorder (DCD) is found in 5%–6% of the pediatric population, defined as poor motor coordination without clear evidence of neurologic pathology (American Psychiatric Association, 2013; Hadders-Algra, 2002). Prevalence rates are higher in those born prematurely (16%). These motor problems interfere with the child's day-to-day function and preacademic performance. Children with DCD comprise a heterogeneous group who manifest what appears to be a borderline form of CP. They have difficulty with gross and fine motor skills, gait and postural control, catching, sensori-perceptual functions (e.g., visuospatial processing), rhythmic coordination, motor planning, and reduced automatization of both movement skills and processing speed. The dysfunctional motor pathways and underlying neural substrate may mimic CP (Blank et al., 2019; Zwicker, Missiuna, Harris, & Boyd, 2012), and it is possible that CP and DCD are on a continuum of neurologic injury, versus being two distinct and separate processes. Many preterm children with DCD display early generalized hypotonia without ataxia (Adams-Chapman et al., 2018). This general change in presentation of motor impairment from severe to mild/moderate may be due to decreased likelihood of macrostructural CNS injury such as Grade III or IV intraventricular hemorrhage; this is replaced by less obvious (and devastating) microcystic and diffuse white matter necrosis.

The Bayley-4 was administered to 40 children identified as motor impaired and this group displayed difficulty on all subscales. The mean Language Composite was 78 and the Motor Composite was 73. The mean Cognitive scaled score was extremely low, while gross motor skills were at the 2nd percentile. It appears that motor deficits have a negative impact on other domains of development, perhaps due to slowed speed of responding, co-occurring visual-perceptual deficits, or the aforementioned poor automatization of motor skills. There is recent evidence that gross motor skills and cognitive development are more highly interrelated than was once thought: the cerebellum and dorsal lateral prefrontal cortex are activated in both cognitive and motor tasks. Hence, motor (particularly gross motor) and cognitive development overlap (Diamond, 2000; Veldman, Santos, Jones, Sousa-Sa, & Okely, 2019) and early problems with motor function may be harbingers of later cognitive issues.

Children with Autism Spectrum Disorder

Autism Spectrum Disorder (ASD) involves impairment in social communication and interaction and the presence of restricted, repetitive behavior, interests, and activities (DSM-5; American Psychiatric Association, 2013). According to the latest CDC data, the incidence of ASD is 1/59, being 4–5 times greater in boys (Baio et al., 2018). Parent report in the National Health Interview Study suggested a 1 in 45 rate (Zablotsky, Black, Maenner, & Schieve, 2015); 31% of children with ASD have IQ/DQs <70, 24% display borderline cognitive skills (70–85), and 45% score>85 at age 8 years (Baio et al., 2018). The median age of diagnosis is approximately 52 months of age, although ASD can be diagnosed as early as 18–24 months, depending on presentation (severity of symptoms). However, mention of developmental concerns by age 36 months was documented for 89% of children with ASD at the 11 CDC sites. It is reported that 86% of the CDC study population meet the autism criteria of both DSM-5 and DSM-IV TR (Baio et al., 2018). In the National Survey of Children's Health, the weighted prevalence of "ever-diagnosed ASD" was

2.79%; it was 2.5% for current ASD (Xu et al., 2018). Children with ASD typically are disadvantaged when compared to peers in regard to language, adaptive, and possibly cognitive development. This is particularly the case if the level of severity is II or III in social communication and interaction (American Psychiatric Association, 2013).

The Bayley-4 was administered to 31 children with ASD (based on DSM-5 criteria). All scores in children with ASD were below controls with Cognitive, Receptive, and Expressive communication being the lowest subscales. The Language Composite standard score was 63, while the Motor Composite was 71 and the Cognitive scaled score was less than the 2nd percentile.

Children with language delay or specific language impairment

Language development is highly variable and progresses as children interact verbally and nonverbally in both receptive and expressive formats. Ten to seventeen percent of young children present with language delays of unknown etiology; these delays being not associated with cognitive, neurologic, sensory, or genetic problems (Bishop, Snowling, Thompson, Greenhalgh, & CATALISE-2 Consortium, 2016; Leonard, 2014). As much as 60% of children with language delay will catch up with their peers by 4 years of age, some spontaneously and others after receiving speech/language interventions (Rescorla, 2011). Approximately 16% of children experience delays in the initial phases of learning language and difficulties will persist in one-half of these children (Feldman, 2019).

Rapin and colleagues (Klein & Rapin, 1990) provide a useful, rather simplistic, three-category classification of developmental language disorders. Group 1 involves output disturbances where there is a problem in expressive language, but comprehension is normal. Phonological disorders that include dysfluencies and articulation problems also fall in this category. Group 2 involves a mixed receptive and expressive disorder. Group 3 includes children with more complex processing disorders—here the content and composition of speech are abnormal. More recently, speech and language problems have been dichotomized into *developmental speech disorders* (DSD; affecting how clearly speech sounds are produced) and *developmental language disorders* (DLD; involving language structure such as grammar and semantics). These often co-occur, but can present independently. DLD is also referred to as a *specific language impairment* (Bishop, Snowling, Thompson, Greenhalgh, & CATALISE-2 Consortium, 2016). In children aged 3–5 years, speech/language impairment is the most frequent reason for enrollment in early childhood education services (Feldman, 2019).

Variations in language development and spontaneous resolution of language problems complicate the diagnosis of Language Delay (LD) and/or Specific Language Impairment (SLI) (also called developmental language disorder; DLD). Nonetheless, early identification of these problems and intervention are vital for improvement (Bishop, Price, Dale, & Plomin, 2003).

In SLI/DLD, mastery of language skills is impaired; this occurs in the absence of intellectual deficits. This disorder occurs in 6%–8% of preschoolers (Tomblin, Smith, & Zhang, 1997; Wallace et al., 2015). Moreover, 50%–70% of these children have another family member with SLI/DLD, suggesting a genetic component (Rice, 2013). Developmentally, these children have a history of being late to talk, experience difficulty learning new words or carrying on a conversation, and as they age, they have particular problems using verbs and the past tense. There may be a discrepancy between nonverbal cognitive ability scores and those that measure language function; children with global developmental delays or intellectual disabilities do not meet criteria for SLI (American Psychiatric Association, 2013). With SLI, language abilities are substantially below those expected for the child's age and may cause functional limitations in communication and social interaction.

Early Language Delay (ELD) is associated with "late talkers" (Rescorla, 2011; Tsybina & Eriks-Brophy, 2007) or "late bloomers," in whom resolution of language deficits typically occurs around the age of 3 years, either spontaneously or in response to brief intervention (LeParo, Justice, Skibbe, & Pianta, 2004). Late talkers, whose prevalence is 10%–15% at 2 years, typically display limited word production (i.e., a vocabulary of less than 50–70 words), few or no word combinations, or are at the 10th percentile or below on parent report of expressive language (Dale, Price, Bishop, & Plomin, 2003; Ellis Weismer & Evans, 2002). Language delay (LD) is typically applied to younger children because it is difficult to accurately diagnose a true *language disorder* prior to age 3.

To summarize, children with speech and language *delays* develop language in the correct sequence, but at a slower rate than would be expected; in contrast, children with a language *disorder* develop language that is qualitatively different from typical development (Wallace et al., 2015). Environmental influences also come into play, with higher maternal education being a protective factor with regard to language development.

The Bayley-4 was administered to 25 children with suspected Language Delay (age range 18–35 months) and 25 children with a Specific Language Impairment (SLI/DLD) (36–42 months). The Language Delay group scored significantly lower than the matched control group on all measures, the Language Composite being 80 and the Motor Composite, 90. Cognitive scores were low average. The highest mean level of performance was on the FM subtest.

With the SLI/DLD group, again all comparisons with controls were statistically significant, and the Language Composite was 82 and the Motor Composite was 85. The Cognitive standard score was borderline.

Children with developmental delay

This group of children is quite heterogeneous. Moreover, it typically is not clear as to whether the problems reflect a temporary lag or a true deficit. Hence, the degree of delay will vary, with some children manifesting minimal concerns, while others may have more significant developmental delays in more than one domain. In order to be included, the infant or toddler must have had an identified developmental delay in two or more of the following areas: cognitive, motor, language, social-emotional, or adaptive functioning; in many of the children this is compatible with the DSM-5 criteria for global developmental delay.

The Bayley-4 was administered to 57 children specifically identified as having developmental delays. Mean scores on all subtests were found to be significantly below comparison children. The mean Cognitive standard score was borderline, while the Language Composite score was 79 and the Motor Composite was 82.

Children with prenatal drug/alcohol exposure

Infants exposed to alcohol prenatally were combined with those exposed to other drugs, because it is virtually impossible to separate the individual differences of any one substance, due to the low probability that exposure would be restricted to only one toxicant in the real world (e.g., Andrews, Davies, Linz, & Payne, 2018). This mode of thinking is in contrast to the "single cause fallacy" where differences between children with prenatal exposure and controls are attributed to one cause (e.g., prenatal opioid exposure) (Larson et al., 2019). Moreover, timing, frequency, amount, and type of drug/alcohol exposure as well as co-exposures cannot be specifically defined in this population and there typically is a lag between birth and the emergence of deficits attributable to such exposures. Therefore, the heterogeneity found in this clinical group is reflective of this population in general.

The CDC reports that 10.2% of pregnant women have consumed alcohol within the last 30 days, while 3.1% have engaged in binge drinking during the same time period (Tan, Denny, Cheal, Sniezek, & Kanny, 2015). Many of these infants have had polydrug exposure in addition to poor prenatal care and prenatal tobacco exposure. This leads to a succession of physical and developmental events. Neurocognitive deficits (in executive function, learning, development, visual-spatial abilities) and poor self-regulation or adaptive function are typically found (Hoyme et al., 2016). There are also interactions between specific genes and fetal drug exposures and evidence that drug combinations (particularly those that include alcohol) are particularly deleterious (Volkow, 2013).

The Bayley-4 was administered to 44 children with a positive history of prenatal drug (cocaine, heroin, methamphetamine, methadone, opioids) or alcohol exposure (FAS, partial FAS, Alcohol Related Neurodevelopmental Disorder (ARND), Fetal Alcohol Spectrum Disorder (FASD), or Neurobehavioral Disorder Associated with Prenatal Alcohol Exposure (ND-PAE); Hoyme et al., 2016). Prenatal exposure to alcohol is frequently associated more with learning disabilities versus generalized cognitive impairment, although both are frequently seen. In children with FAS, the average cognitive score is in the 65–72 range; those without dysmorphic features have an average intellectual score in the mid-80s. Executive functions also are often affected (Pelligrino & Pelligrino, 2008). These children often have ADHD and early tendencies suggestive of this disorder may be evident when the Bayley-4 is administered to toddlers.

Infants and toddlers with prenatal drug exposure scored significantly below matched peers on all measures. The mean Language Composite was 81, while the Motor Composite was 83; the Cognitive standard score was at the 5th percentile.

Children born premature

Infants born <28 weeks of gestation are classified as extremely preterm (EPT), those born 28–31 weeks very preterm (VPT), 32–33 weeks moderate preterm (MPT), and 34–36 weeks, late preterm (LPT; previously called "near term" until 2005). Approximately 105,000 babies are born each year VPT and EPT, the latter comprising 1%–2% of all births

(Johnson & Marlow, 2017). Seventy five percent of preterm births fall in the LPT group, and despite more maturation than those born EPT or VPT, these children still tend to have developmental outcome scores that are below their full-term peers (Mc Gowan, Aldirice, Holmes, & Johnson, 2011). In general, the smaller or younger the infant, the lower the mean group DQ/IQ. For each week of gestational age <32 weeks, the average decline in IQ scores is 1.5–2.5 points (Kerr-Wilson, Mackay, Smith, & Pell, 2011; Marlow, Wolke, Bracewell, & Samara, 2005). This same gradient of increasing problems is found with later academic achievement, visual-motor skills, language, and neuropsychological functions (Aylward, 2002, 2005). MPT children do more poorly with respect to cognitive and attentional skills than do older preterms. For the Bayley-4 clinical group analyses, those born preterm were placed in two separate groups: Very/Extremely Preterm (<32 weeks) and Moderate/Late Preterm (32 through 36 weeks).

In order to identify more "typical" preterm infants, those with less severe but frequently seen conditions such as respiratory distress syndrome, apnea/bradycardia, mild IVH (Grades I or II), or hyperbilirubinemia were included. Premature infants with more severe conditions as well as those born small for gestational age were excluded.

The Bayley-4 was administered to 70 children born moderate to late preterm and 66 children born very to extremely preterm.

Children born extremely or very preterm (<32 weeks) scored below their matched controls in all comparisons. The Language Composite was 86, while the Motor Composite was 79. The Cognitive standard score was approximately 1 SD below average. These infants also scored below their Moderate/late preterm peers. Comparing the children born Moderate/Late premature to their controls again showed significant differences in all areas, although their scores were not as low as the children born at younger gestational ages. Most scores were low average; the Language Composite was 93, and Motor, 90. These findings are compatible to the current literature where 16% of children born EPT or VPT had later IQs that were 2 standard deviations below average, versus a rate of 2.5% in those born full-term (Twilhaar et al., 2018).

To summarize the clinical validity data, the Bayley-4 discriminates at-risk infants from their matched peers in all the clinical samples surveyed.

CHAPTER 12

The Bayley-4 on Q-global

Andre C. Lane
Associate Research Director, Pearson, San Antonio, TX,
The United States of America

Contents

Bayley 4 Clinical Use and Interpretation
https://doi.org/10.1016/B978-0-12-817754-9.00012-X

Introduction

The Bayley-4 on Q-global (B4QG) adds a unique dimension to developmental assessment and facilitates administration and scoring of the Cognitive, Receptive Communication, Expressive Communication, Fine Motor, and Gross Motor subtests of the Bayley-4. It can be used on any device with internet access including desktops, laptops, tablets, and other mobile devices. The B4QG combines portions of the Bayley-4 Record Form and Administration Manual for easier availability during testing and more efficient administration and scoring. Examiners can also review responses prior to submitting the assessment to Q-global for scoring and reporting.

Objectives of the Bayley-4 on Q-global

The two primary objectives of the B4QG were to: (a) reduce testing time; and (b) reduce the complexity of administration and scoring.

Reduce testing time

A Bayley-4 goal was to reduce the testing time to approximately 30 minutes for ages 1–12 months and a maximum of 70 minutes for ages 13–42 months. The B4QG reduces preparation and item administration time, thereby addressing this goal. In addition, the B4QG programmatically determines the age of the child based on information entered into Q-global and adjusts for prematurity. Using the expected and actual birth date, the B4QG automatically navigates to the correct starting point for each subtest. Basal and ceiling criteria are tracked and notification is provided when the reverse rule needs to be applied or the discontinue rule has been met.

Reduce the complexity of administration and scoring

The B4QG reduces administration complexity by including a user interface that incorporates all elements needed to administer the item without the need for a separate manual. For each item, the materials needed, position of the child, item instructions, and the specific text to be spoken by the examiner are displayed. An integrated timer or stopwatch eliminates the need to handle a physical timing device and on some items provides an item score suggestion when the timer is stopped.

Linear versus nonlinear administration

Assessments similar to the Bayley-4 are intended to be administered and scored as part of a linear administration. Linear means that the first item administered to the child is set by chronological age. A basal is established and items are administered in sequential order until the discontinue rule is met or the last item of the subtest is given. Linear assessments are standardized in this manner and the results are considered invalid if the procedures are not followed. The linear administration procedure has two prime advantages: (a) assurance that all appropriate items are administered; and (b) scaled scores and standard scores can be derived. Linear administrations also ensure that the testing procedures are consistent with those used during standardization. However, linear administration mandates a rigid test administration style that can be disruptive to rapport building, resulting in invalid test results due to noncompliance. Testing time may also be longer and a linear administration on a digital application prohibits recording and scoring of items that are observation-based until the item comes up in the sequential order.

A nonlinear approach has the same requirements as the linear administration (e.g., start points, basals, ceilings), but is more flexible, permitting items and subtests to be administered in the order that best suits the child. For example, in a nonlinear administration, the start point is determined by the child's age and an attempt is made to establish the basal; however, if the caregiver spontaneously begins to describe the child's behaviors that correspond to an item much later in the item set or even in another subtest, a nonlinear administration allows that item to be scored before the basal is established. Furthermore, a nonlinear administration allows the flexibility to administer similar items that use the same test materials sequentially. The B4QG is designed to accommodate both a linear and nonlinear administration approach.

The Bayley-4 on Q-global navigation

Start screen

When the B4QG is launched, the start screen allows for adjustment for prematurity. The *Test Age* is determined by the information entered in Q-global prior to launching the assessment. Select *Yes or No* under *Adjustment for Prematurity?* (A in Fig. 12.1). If adjustment for prematurity is needed, the expected birth date should be entered (B in Fig. 12.1) to determine the *Adjusted Test Age* (C in Fig. 12.1).

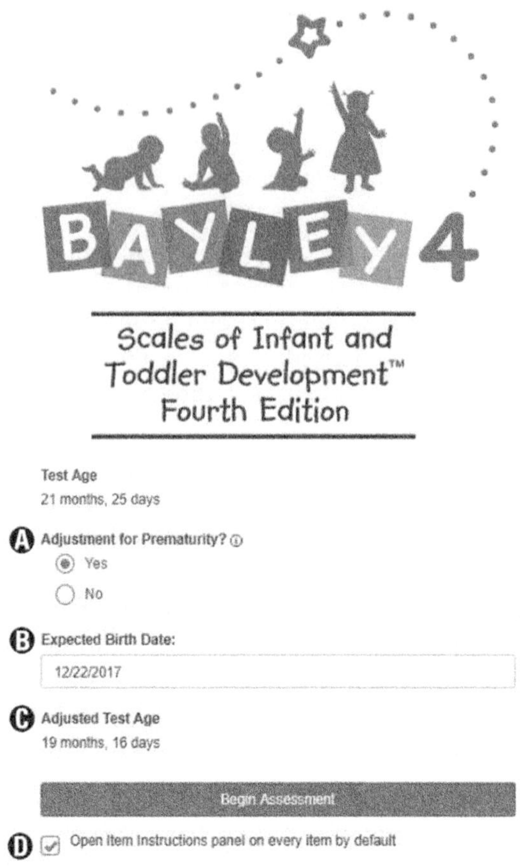

Fig. 12.1 Start screen.

The start screen also allows for the selection of a default setting for the *Item Instructions* panel (D in Fig. 12.1). When first learning the Bayley-4, it is advantageous to have the *Item Instructions* automatically open when selecting an item. However, once familiarity with the items is established, the panel default can be modified by deselecting the checkbox. Once the assessment begins, the start screen cannot be accessed or modified.

Subtest and Review tabs

The B4QG includes the five subtest tabs and the *Review* tab (A in Fig. 12.2). After the *Begin Assessment* button has been selected, the B4QG navigates to the *Cognitive* tab, but subtest and *Review* tabs can be selected any time. Selecting a subtest tab navigates to the start point item for the child even when other items before or after the start point have been scored.

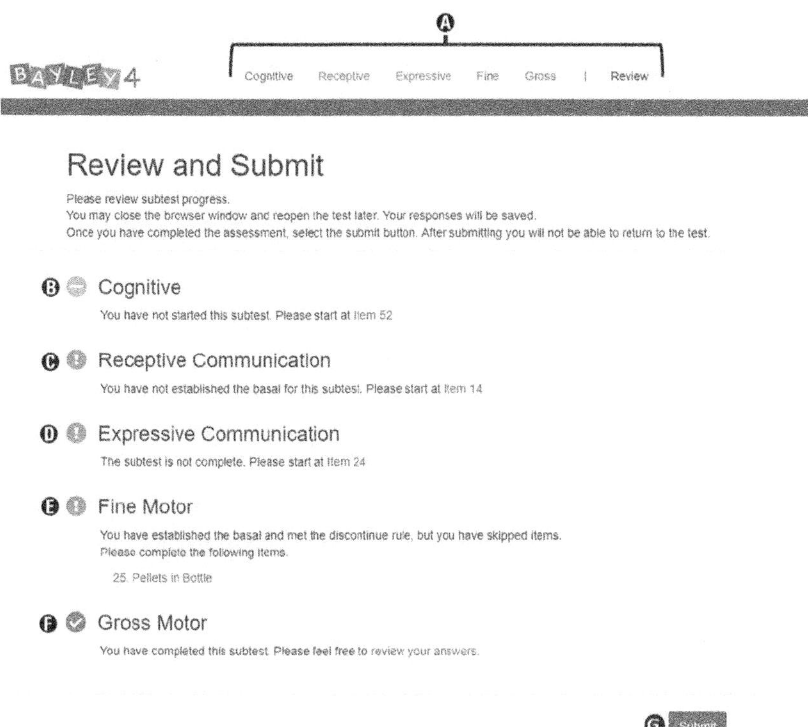

Fig. 12.2 Subtest and Review tabs.

On the *Review* tab, subtests are initially shown as not started (B in Fig. 12.2). As items are scored, the subtest status icon adjusts to reflect what is occurring during testing, such as the need to establish a basal (C in Fig. 12.2), which item needs to be administered next in order to complete the subtest (D in Fig. 12.2) and skipped items (E in Fig. 12.2). When at least one subtest is completed (F in Fig. 12.2), the *Submit* button is available (G in Fig. 12.2). Once the *Submit* button is selected, it is not possible to return to the subtest tabs, but all submitted data are available in Q-global.

Items panel

The items panel displays all items for a subtest and can be used to move among the item set. This panel also contains all start point icons for the Bayley-4 age range (A in Fig. 12.3). Each item is designated by an item number and title and, when selected, is made more visible by a lighter shading (B in Fig. 12.3). A blue or gray indicator next to the item means an item score has been assigned and saved. A blue indicator (light gray in

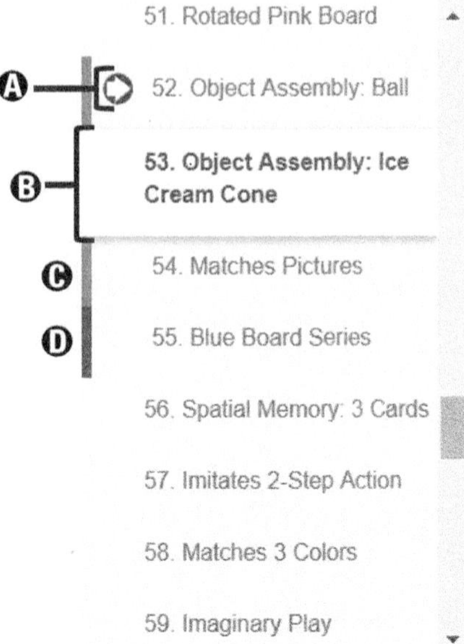

Fig. 12.3 Items panel.

figure; C in Fig. 12.3) means the score is either a 1 or 2; a gray indicator corresponds to a score of 0 (D in Fig. 12.3). These indicators can be used to manually track the reverse and discontinue rule and allow skipped items to be quickly identified.

Filters

Beneath the items panel is a section that contains various filters (A in Fig. 12.4). The initial default view is the *All* filtered view. This allows all items of a subtest to be displayed in the items panel. During testing, behavioral observations may be made which allow the scores for certain items to be assigned. These items can be scored at any time using the *Obs* filter. In some circumstances, such as when scoring items based on observations made when the child and caregiver are first met, it may be more appropriate to use the Bayley-4 Observation Checklist and subsequently use the *Obs* filter to locate and assign scores.

When a related items filter is present (e.g., Blocks and cups), it appears under the *All* filter (B in Fig. 12.4). Two related items filters will never appear at the same time. These filters function in the same way as the *Obs*

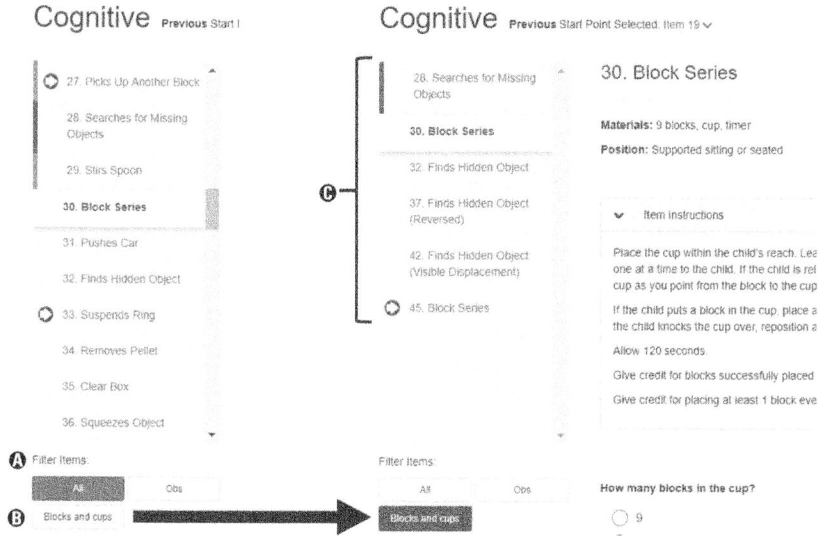

Fig. 12.4 Filters.

filter, displaying only items associated with the filter (C in Fig. 12.4). If the item selected before a filter is selected is not part of the items in the filter, either the next unadministered item after the start point in the filtered view is displayed or the first item in the subtest is displayed, whichever is appropriate.

If a filter is used in more than one subtest (A in Fig. 12.5), the filtered view will be maintained after moving to another subtest. For example, in Fig. 12.5, the *Ring with string* filter is selected and the three items in the filter from the Cognitive subtest have been scored. When the *Fine Motor* tab is selected, the items using the Ring with string from the Fine Motor subtest are now displayed (B in Fig. 12.5). This decreases testing duration time and maintains optimal rapport and workflow. The full utility of the filters may only be realized after becoming familiar with the Bayley-4 and mastering many of the test administration mechanics.

Next Item button

When the *Next Item* button (see Fig. 12.6) is selected, the next unadministered item in the subtest appears or the start point item for the next subtest if it is at the end of a subtest. Responses, scores, and other information associated with the item are saved when: (a) the *Next Item* button is selected; (b) when selecting another item in the items panel; or (c) when selecting a subtest tab or the *Review tab*.

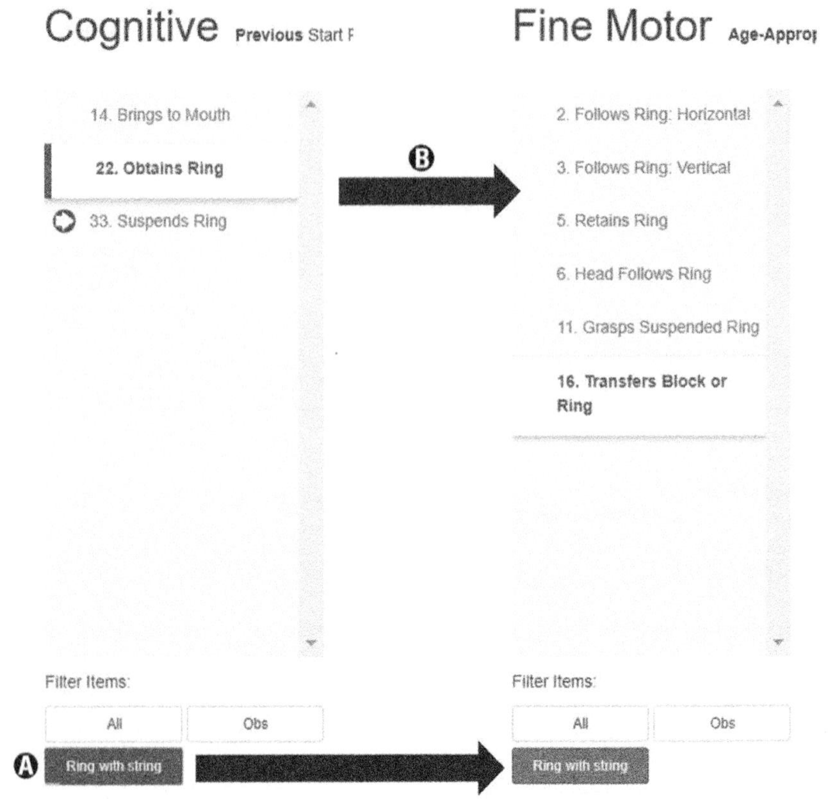

Cognitive Previous Start F

14. Brings to Mouth
22. Obtains Ring
33. Suspends Ring

Filter Items:
All | Obs
Ring with string

Fine Motor Age-Appro

2. Follows Ring: Horizontal
3. Follows Ring: Vertical
5. Retains Ring
6. Head Follows Ring
11. Grasps Suspended Ring
16. Transfers Block or Ring

Filter Items:
All | Obs
Ring with string

A B

Fig. 12.5 Example of related items filter.

Fig. 12.6 Next Item button.

The Bayley-4 on Q-global administration rules

Start points

The start point item can be viewed in two locations (A and B in Fig. 12.7). Depending on the device used, the age range associated with a start point can be displayed by selecting or hovering over the start point icon.

The *Start Point Selected* drop-down menu (B in Fig. 12.7) includes both the age-appropriate start point and the previous start point (C and D in Fig. 12.7). When a perfect score on the child's age-appropriate start point item is unlikely, the *Start Point Selected* drop-down menu should be used

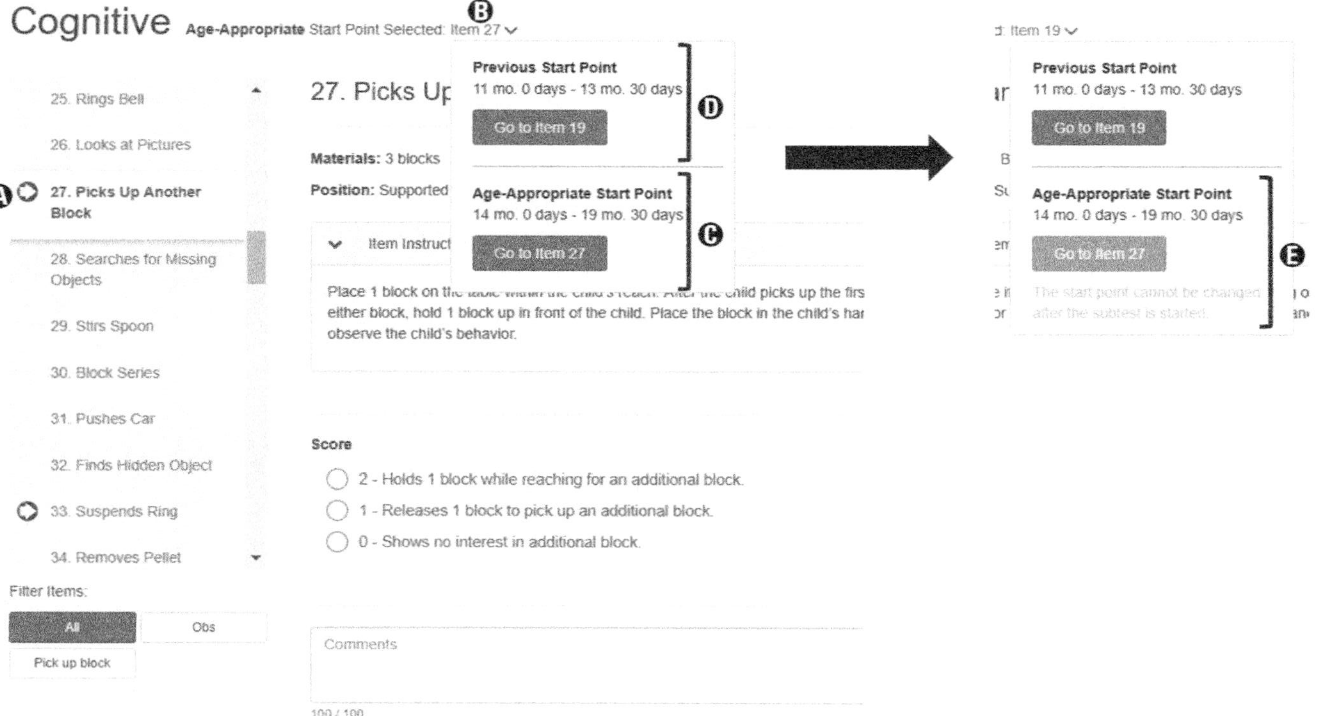

Fig. 12.7 Start Points.

to start at the previous start point. Once the *Previous Start Point* or *Age-Appropriate Start Point* is selected and at least one score for that subtest is saved, the unselected start point button is disabled (E in Fig. 12.7).

If the *Previous Start Point* is selected after at least one score for that subtest is saved, the Previous Start Point pop up is displayed (see Fig. 12.8). If *Yes* is selected, the *Age-Appropriate Start Point* button is disabled (E in Fig. 12.7). All previously saved data will be preserved, but the basal will need to be established at the previous start point.

Reverse rule

To establish the basal, a score of 2 on the start point item and the two items immediately following need to be obtained. This is the same for all five subtests. If the child is assigned a score of 0 or 1 on either the start point item or the two items after the start point item, the Reverse pop up will be displayed (see Fig. 12.9).

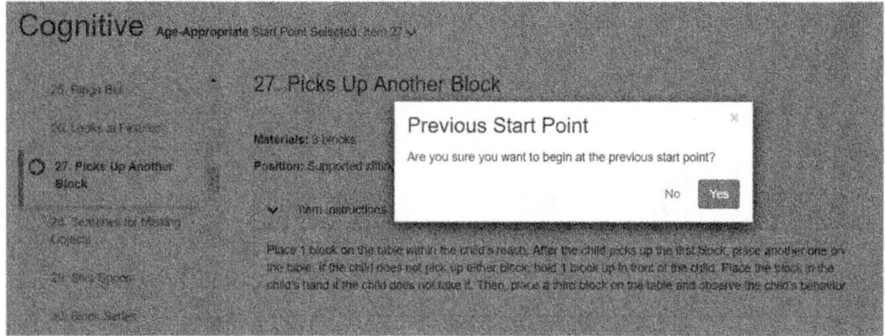

Fig. 12.8 Previous Start Point pop.

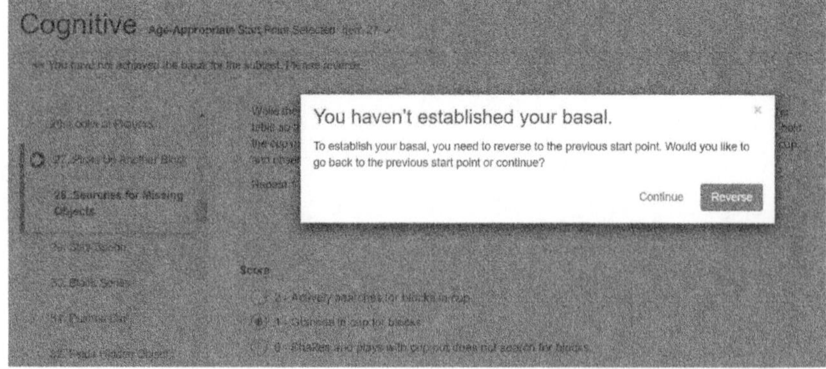

Fig. 12.9 Reverse pop up.

The pop up contains two buttons, *Continue* and *Reverse*. If *Continue* is selected, the next unadministered item appears; with *Reverse*, the assessment navigates to the previous start point item. The Reverse pop up will only appear once per subtest. After reversing to the previous start point, if the child still does not obtain a score of 2 on the start point item or either of the two subsequent items, the Reverse panel is activated and remains at the top of the screen under the subtest name until the basal has been established (see Fig. 12.10). The Reverse panel link is helpful when scoring other items prior to establishing the basal (e.g., scoring Observations items).

Discontinue rule

The Discontinue pop up and panel function much like the Reverse pop up and panel. Once five consecutive scores of 0 are obtained on a subtest, the Discontinue pop up will appear (see Fig. 12.11).

If the *Next Item* button is selected, the next unadministered item appears. If the *Discontinue* button is selected, the assessment will navigate to the start point item for the next subtest or to the *Review* tab. The Discontinue pop up will only appear once per subtest, but the Discontinue panel will remain at the top of the screen under the subtest name (see Fig. 12.12) to allow navigation to the next appropriate item. Even when the subtest discontinue rule has been met and the *Discontinue* button or the link in the Discontinue

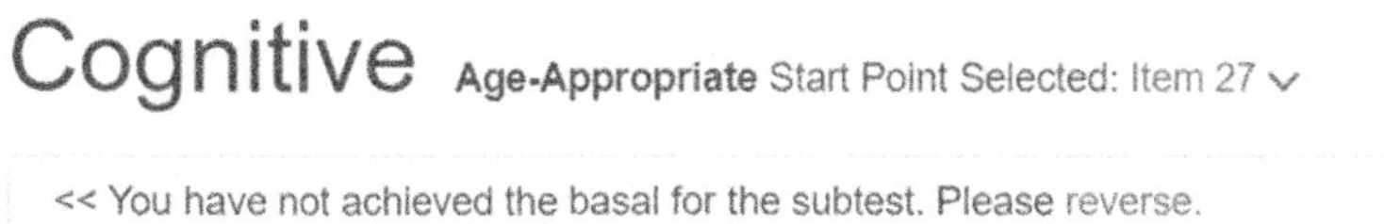

Fig. 12.10 Reverse panel.

Fig. 12.11 Discontinue pop up.

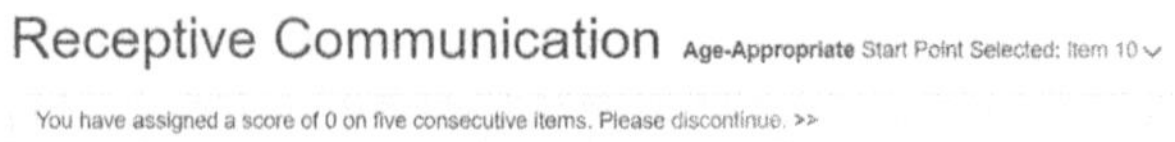

Receptive Communication Age-Appropriate Start Point Selected: Item 10

You have assigned a score of 0 on five consecutive items. Please discontinue. >>

Fig. 12.12 Discontinue panel.

panel has been selected, navigation to complete subtests using the subtest and *Review* tabs is possible. This can be helpful when testing the limits.

The Bayley-4 on Q-global item interface

Materials and Position

Materials needed for an item and the recommended position of the child appear under the *Materials* and *Position* section at the top of each item (A in Fig. 12.13).

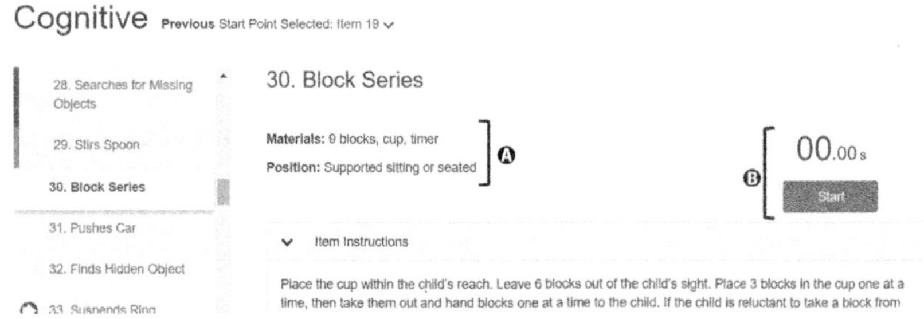

Fig. 12.13 Materials, Position, and timer or stopwatch.

Timer and stopwatch

The timer or stopwatch is located to the right of the *Materials* and *Position* section when needed (B in Fig. 12.13). The timer and stopwatch have slightly different functionality. The timer is used to score the item and a stopwatch is provided when stimuli are presented for a specific amount of time or an item has a time element.

Timer

Use the *Start and Stop* buttons (A and B in Fig. 12.14) to start and stop the timer. For those items with a time limit, the numerals turn red once the time limit has been reached.

Fig. 12.14 Start and Stop buttons.

Once the timer or stopwatch is stopped, minus and plus buttons appear (see Fig. 12.15). When one of these buttons is selected, the numbers in the timer will increment in 1-second intervals until the button is selected again.

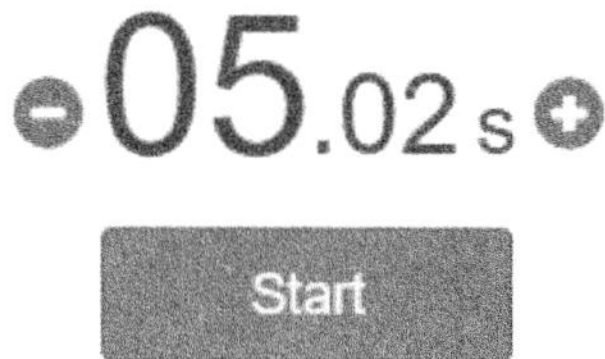

Fig. 12.15 Minus and plus buttons.

For items that have both a response that can be selected and a timer, the response radio buttons are disabled as a reminder to stop the timer. Nonetheless, the item score radio buttons can be selected even while the timer is running.

Stopwatch

The stopwatch includes many of the same features as the timer and offers a *Reset* button (A in Fig. 12.16). When the *Reset* button is selected, the time displayed is reset to zero seconds. This is particularly helpful when an item has more than one trial.

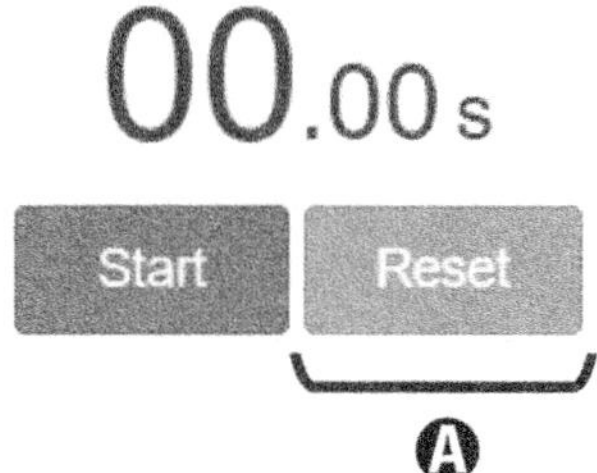

Fig. 12.16 Reset button.

Item Instructions

The *Item Instructions* panel contains item administration and scoring directions and other instructions. This panel can be opened and closed by selecting the arrow (A in Fig. 12.17).

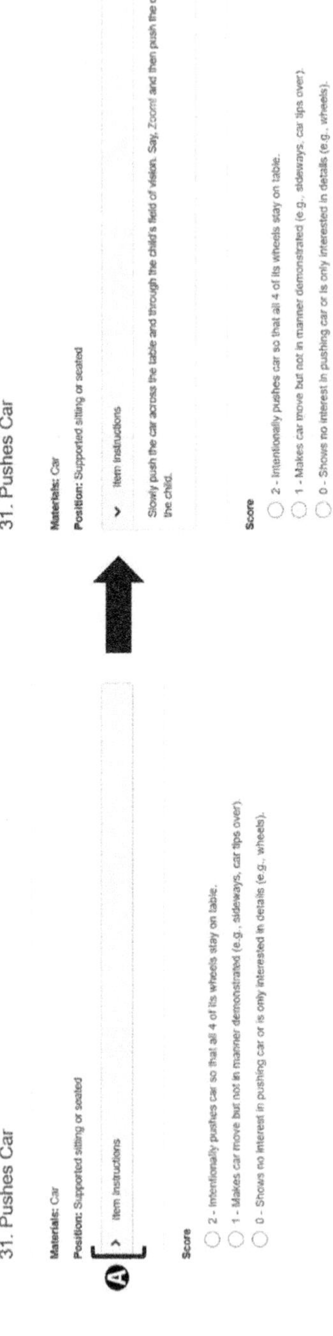

Fig. 12.17 Example of Item Instructions.

Art

For some items, art is included in the *Item Instructions* panel (see Fig. 12.18). An image of the Stimulus Book or Response Booklet is shown when either is required. For other items, art is included to help with scoring.

Item text

For each item, instructions are in black color (A in Fig. 12.19), while text spoken to the child is in blue (B and C in Fig. 12.19).

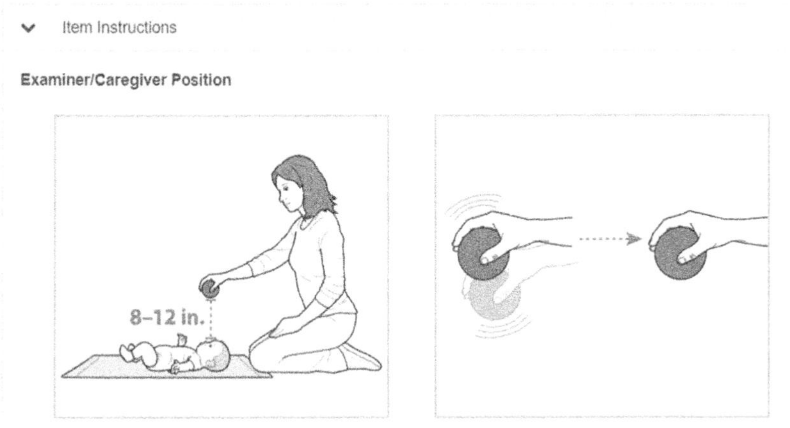

Fig. 12.18 Example of art in the Item Instructions panel.

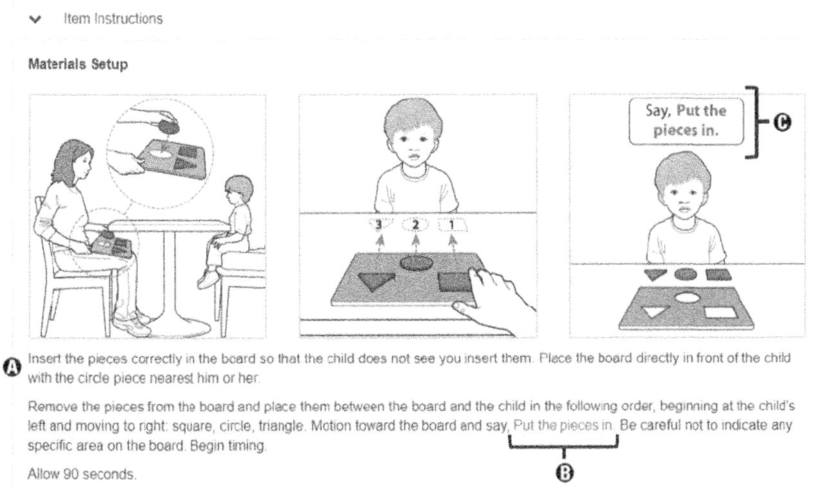

Fig. 12.19 Example of item text.

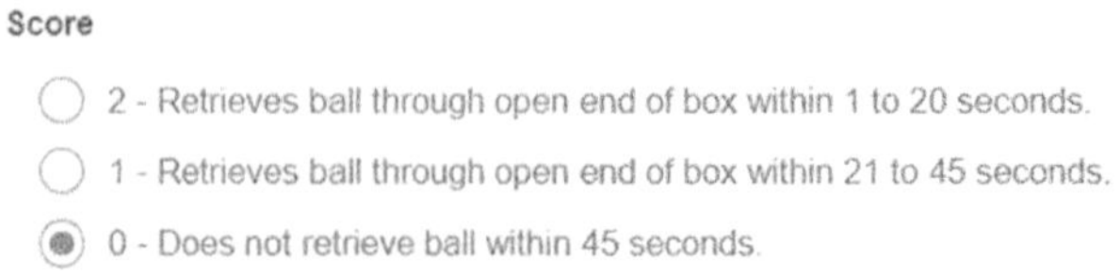

Score

- ◯ 2 - Retrieves ball through open end of box within 1 to 20 seconds.
- ◯ 1 - Retrieves ball through open end of box within 21 to 45 seconds.
- ◉ 0 - Does not retrieve ball within 45 seconds.

Fig. 12.20 Example of Score section.

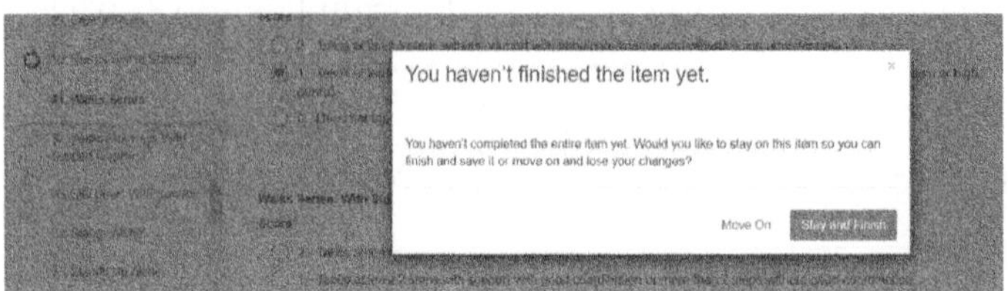

Fig. 12.21 Stay and Finish pop up.

Score section

The radio button or the text is selected in the *Score* section to assign a score (see Fig. 12.20).

If the item is not complete, a Stay and Finish pop up appears (see Fig. 12.21). If the *Move On* button is selected, the next unadministered item appears. If the *Stay and Finish* button is selected, the assessment returns to the current item.

Comments section

A section is provided for notes or verbatim responses to be recorded for each item. The maximum number of characters that can be entered is 100.

The Bayley-4 on Q-global item types

Item with multiple trials

For some items, there is a section for recording the child's trial responses. Each trial has a label (A in Fig. 12.22) and two buttons. When the check mark button (i.e., correct) is selected, the button turns green (B in Fig. 12.22); when the X button (i.e., incorrect) is selected, it turns red (C in Fig. 12.22). If a button is accidentally selected, it can be changed. Once the minimum number of correct trial responses needed for a maximum score is obtained, an alert is provided (D in Fig. 12.22).

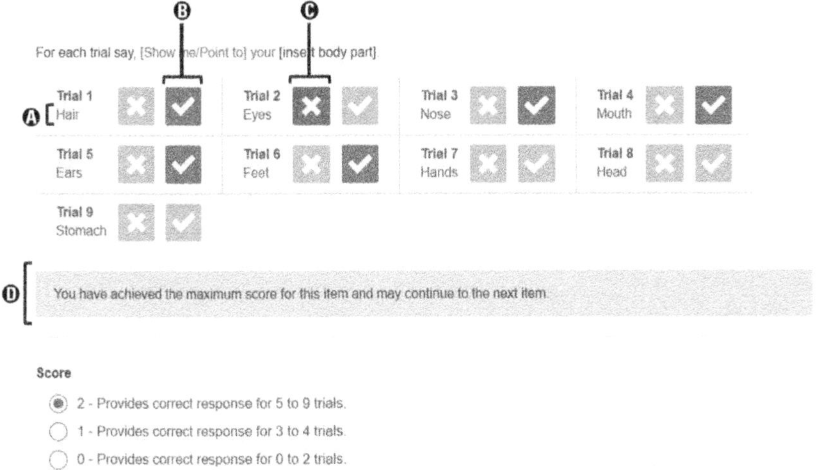

Fig. 12.22 Example of item with multiple trials.

Cognitive Item 81. Completes Patterns has a feature that guides recording and scoring the trials in different manner: once the score for the first trial is selected (i.e., correct/incorrect), the next trial is brought to the center of the screen. A score suggestion is made after the last trial is scored.

Series items

The series items differ in that they are administered just once, but scored in multiple places. A number of different series item types are used in the B4QG.

Response-based series items

A basic feature of the series item design is the ability to score all items in the series with the selection of a single response. For example, the Block Stacking Series requires the child to stack blocks and the number of blocks is recorded (A in Fig. 12.23). When the response is selected, an item score suggestion is made for all three items in the series (B in Fig. 12.23). If a selection is made inadvertently, another response can be selected, and the score suggestions for all items will adjust automatically. In this example, the scores are saved in three locations in the items panel (A–C in Fig. 12.24).

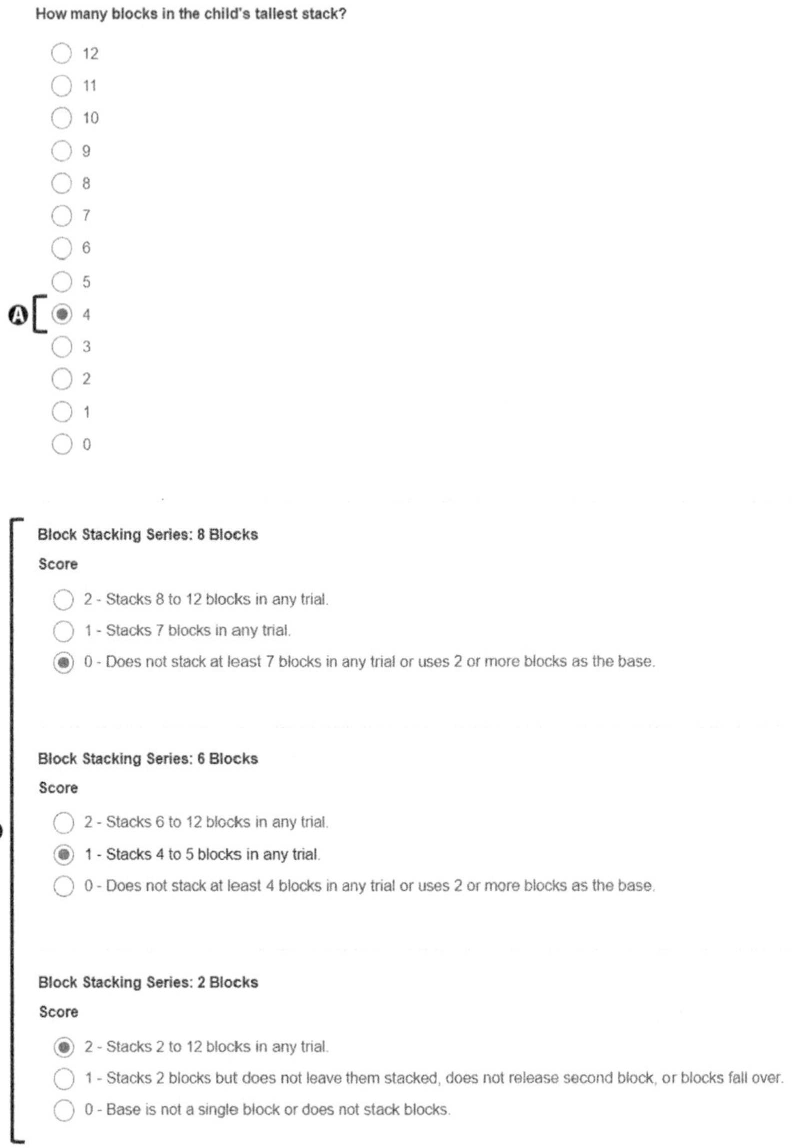

Fig. 12.23 Example of response-based series item.

Timer-based series items

In Fig. 12.25, the timer was stopped at 17 seconds (A in Fig. 12.25). Therefore, one point was assigned for the Supported Sitting Series: 30 Seconds item (B in Fig. 12.25), and two points were assigned for the Supported Sitting Series: 10 Seconds item (C in Fig. 12.25).

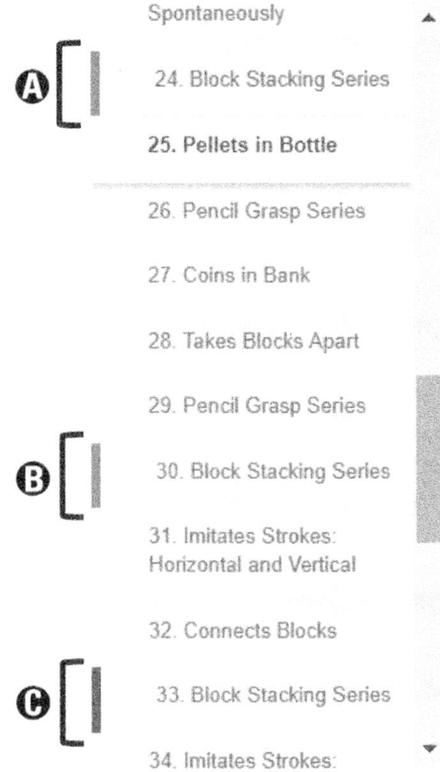

Fig. 12.24 Example of series items in the items panel.

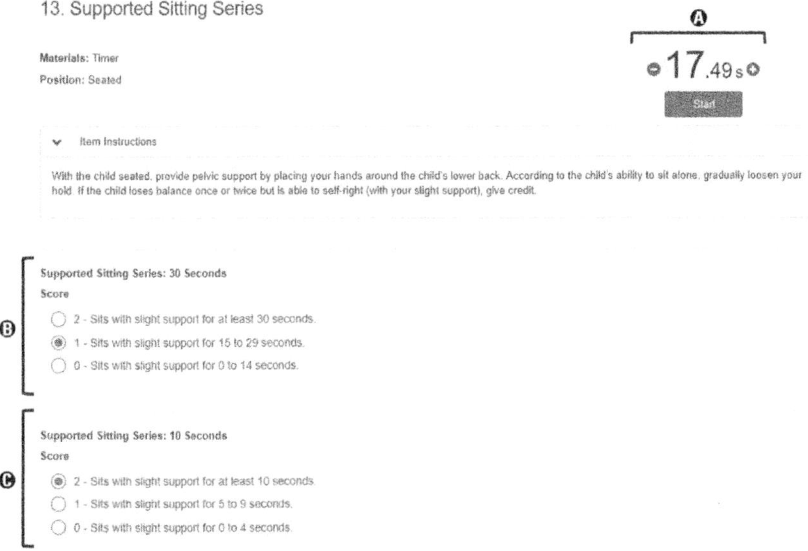

Fig. 12.25 Example of timer-based series item.

Response- and timer-based series items

In Fig. 12.26, the timer was stopped at 41 seconds (A in Fig. 12.26). Three pieces were placed in the board (B in Fig. 12.26), so two points were assigned for the Pink Board Series: 3 Pieces item (C in Fig. 12.26), and two points were assigned for the Pink Board Series: 2 Pieces item (D in Fig. 12.26).

Multitrial series items

A subset of series items has multiple trials (see Fig. 12.27). As trials are scored, item score suggestions are made simultaneously. An alert appears when the minimum number of correct trial responses needed is obtained.

Image-based series items

In Fig. 12.28, the partial thumb opposition grasp was selected and scores were assigned accordingly.

Items with caregiver questions

The caregiver questions do not have to be asked every time they are presented, but the B4QG supports the administration and scoring of those items when needed. The caregiver question appears outside the *Item Instructions* panel (A in Fig. 12.29). Radio buttons in the *Score* section are used to score

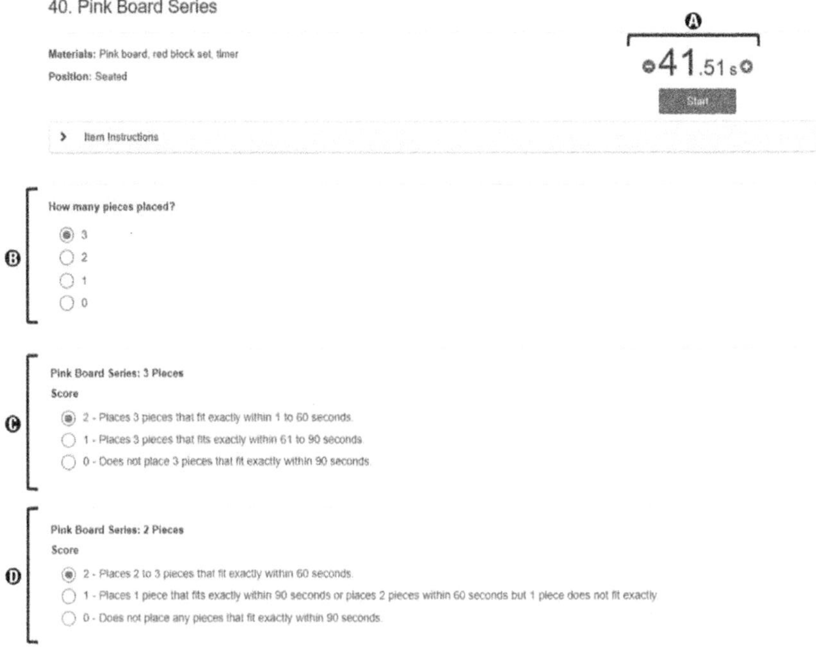

Fig. 12.26 Example of response- and timer-based series item.

For each trial say, Show me the baby's [insert body part].

You have achieved the maximum score for this item and may continue to the next item.

Parts of Doll Series: 5 Correct

Score

- (●) 2 - Provides correct response for 5 to 9 trials.
- ( ) 1 - Provides correct response for 3 to 4 trials.
- ( ) 0 - Provides correct response for 0 to 2 trials.

Parts of Doll Series: 2 Correct

Score

- (●) 2 - Provides correct response for 2 to 9 trials.
- ( ) 1 - Provides correct response for 1 trial.
- ( ) 0 - Provides correct response for 0 trials.

Fig. 12.27 Example of multitrial series item.

Please select image that best represents grasp.

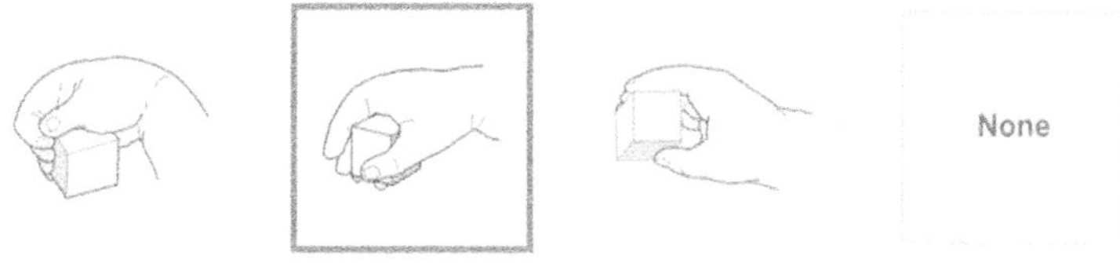

Block Grasp Series: Thumb-Fingertip

Score

- ( ) 2 - Grasps block using thumb-fingertip grasp.
- (●) 1 - Grasps block using partial thumb opposition grasp.
- ( ) 0 - Uses less advanced grasp.

Block Grasp Series: Whole Hand

Score

- (●) 2 - Grasps block using 1 hand with whole hand (palmar) grasp or uses more advanced grasp.
- ( ) 1 - Grasps block using both hands.
- ( ) 0 - Does not grasp block.

Fig. 12.28 Example of image-based series item.

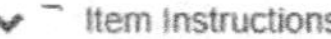

Fig. 12.29 Example of caregiver question.

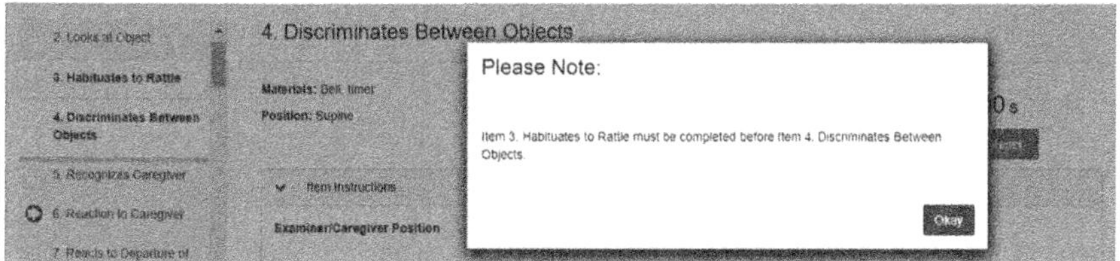

Fig. 12.30 Example of paired items message.

either the structured item or the caregiver question and the scoring criteria is separated by the pipe character (B in Fig. 12.29). Place a checkmark to indicate that the caregiver question was asked and used to score the item (C in Fig. 12.29).

Shared items

Six items are shared between the Cognitive and Receptive Communication subtests. The assessment automatically saves the assigned score in both subtests once the item is complete.

Paired items

There are several items that can be scored after a prerequisite item has been scored. If the prerequisite item has not been scored, an alert will display (see Fig. 12.30). When the *Okay* button is selected, the assessment navigates to the appropriate item.

Summary

This chapter provides a brief overview of the B4QG. Additional information can be found in the Bayley-4 Digital Administration User's Guide and the Bayley-4 Administration and Technical Manuals. Readers are encouraged to review these material as well.

CHAPTER 13

Sample cases

Contents

This chapter includes examples of application of the Bayley-4 to additional clinical cases. These cases were selected to provide the examiner with more variety integrating Bayley-4 findings with historical and demographic information and in providing feedback to caregivers.

Case 1: Maria

Maria is a 2-year, 14-day-old female who was referred for developmental testing by her primary care physician. Her parents were concerned that when compared to her 4½ year old sister, she was consistently slower to develop over the first 2 years. No area of particular weakness was indicated, with Maria's parents stating that she was "pretty much slow in everything." The toddler has been in good physical health over the last 2 years. She was born at 38 weeks gestation and her birth history was unremarkable, with Apgars of 7 and 8 at 1 and 5 minutes, respectively.

Bayley 4 Clinical Use and Interpretation
https://doi.org/10.1016/B978-0-12-817754-9.00013-1

According to parent report, Maria's PCP mentioned low tone at the 9-month well baby check, with "slip through" when she was held vertically under the armpits. She also did not support her weight when standing, but this eventually improved. Because of this gradual improvement, nothing was done about the decreased tone. Developmental milestones were always at the high end of normal to mildly delayed. Currently, Maria readily makes eye contact, responds to her name, smiles, and seeks attention. Maria likes to be in the company of her sister. She was irritable during the first several months after birth and would not sleep through the night until recently. The family's income and education place them in the upper middle SES range.

Maria was given the Bayley-4 cognitive, language, motor, and adaptive scales. The social emotional scale was not completed in this evaluation because social emotional functioning was not a concern, but time was.

Findings: (Level I)

On the Bayley-4, Maria obtained a Cognitive scale score of 7 (16th percentile, borderline range). Her resulting Cognitive Composite score was 85 (95% confidence interval 78–94), suggesting low average to borderline functioning. Overall, Maria's cognitive performance was noted to be at a 19-month age equivalent. When considering percent delay, there is a 5-month lag that equates to approximately a 20% delay in this domain.

The toddler obtained a Receptive Communication scaled score of 7 (16th percentile; borderline) and an Expressive Communication scaled score of 6 (9th percentile; borderline). The obtained age equivalents were 18 and 17 months, which are approximately 6 and 7 months below her chronologic age, respectively. The Language Composite was 79 (8th percentile; 95% CI 73–85), this falling in the low average to borderline range (considering the 95% CI). This score is approximately 1.3 standard deviations below average. Maria's receptive communication skills were delayed by 25% (18 months/24 months), while her expressive skills were 29% delayed (17/24 months).

Maria obtained a Fine Motor scale score of 8 (25th percentile; low average) and a Gross Motor scale score of 6 (9th percentile; borderline); these correspond to 21-month and a 16-month age equivalents, respectively. The Motor Composite standard score was 82 (12th percentile; 76–91); this score also falling in the borderline to low average range (> 1 SD below average). The young lady's fine motor skills were 5 months delayed (21 months/24 months = 12%), while gross motor skills were 9 months below her current age (33% delayed).

Finally, with respect to Adaptive function, Maria received a Bayley-4 Adaptive Behavior Composite of 83, this being in the low average range. Her lowest score was obtained in the Communication Domain (70; 2nd percentile), with expressive skills being lower than receptive abilities. The Daily Living (85; 16th percentile) and Social (88; 21st percentile) standard scores were in the low average range.

Level II

Comparison of subtest scaled scores revealed Communication to be a major problem. The ASD Checklist had very few positive indicators, essentially eliminating autism as a likely cause for the parents' concerns. As was indicated in the Level I interpretation, percent delay (a rather imprecise metric) ranged from 12% to 33%, based on estimated age equivalents that spanned the 16–21-month age range. Fine motor skills were most developed, while gross motor abilities and expressive communication skills were least mature.

Level III: (Synthesis and discussion)

Gross motor function is an area of relative concern, with 90% of the children of Maria's age doing better. This may also qualify her for EI services (physical therapy), given that her state requires a 30% or more delay in one or more areas of function. This motor concern ties into earlier findings of low tone noted at 9 months. When Maria runs, she tends to take short, rather stiff steps, and does not move her arms in a coordinated fashion. She also cannot jump from the floor or bottom step with both feet leaving the surface simultaneously. The possibility of a developmental coordination disorder is raised. Of note is that borderline to low average functioning was found in other areas as well, and if this pattern persists, a diagnosis of global developmental delay may be entertained. It is concerning that language also is below average as this is highly correlated with later cognitive abilities and there is ample language stimulation provided in the home, ruling out the home environment as a potential risk factor for the language problems. Hence, the parents are faced with the conundrum of whether Maria is displaying emerging skills that are delayed, or if she has mild, more persistent deficits.

Without doubt, Maria would also benefit from early speech/language intervention. Children who display developmental profiles similar to Maria's are the ones who derive most benefit from Early Intervention because the magnitude of delay is not overwhelming and no extremely low ceiling is imposed due to biological causes. Fine motor function and adaptive skills are areas of relative strength. To address the question regarding whether Maria is displaying delays (with anticipated catch-up) or a more serious deficit, follow-up testing in 6 months is recommended. Serial testing will also allow documentation of improvement or lack of such after provision of intervention services.

Case 2: Aaron

Aaron is a 6-month, 10-day-old boy with Down Syndrome. He is in Early Intervention and receives developmental therapy, physical/occupational therapy, and speech/language services on a weekly basis due to his established risk designation. Aaron is also enrolled in a hospital-based follow-up program for infants at biological or established risk. Children are seen in this clinic at the age of 6 months (corrected age if preterm) for their first visit and are given the Bayley-4. Aaron's parents are anxious to see where he is developmentally. He has had cardiac issues that have been addressed, but which continue to need close monitoring. Aaron also has had some feeding issues that are being handled by the speech/language specialist. The youngster does not babble, and he doesn't respond consistently to voices or sounds. His parents and the physical therapist suggest that his tone is "floppy," and he currently cannot sit without a great deal of support.

Findings: (Level I)

Aaron received a Bayley-4 Cognitive scale score of 8 (25th percentile). His Cognitive Composite score was 90 (25th percentile: 95% CI ±7), placing him in the low average-to-average range. The raw score equates to a 5-month, 10-day age equivalent, indicating a 1-month delay (16%).

The infant's Receptive Communication scale score was 5 (5th percentile; extremely low), this being at a 3-month, 10-day age equivalent; his Expressive Communication scale score was 2 (1st percentile; < 16-day age level). This score was also extremely low. Many of the receptive items involved his reaction to sound, where Aaron received scores of "1." This is indicative of emerging skills, but these were inconsistent. Expressively, he was social (e.g., smiling), but produced few vocalizations. As a result, he demonstrated greater than a 90% delay in this domain (16 days/250 days). The overall Language Composite was 63 (1st percentile; 95% CI ±7). Aaron's performance falls in the extremely low range (although the CI barely includes borderline scores).

The Fine Motor scaled score was extremely low (5; 5th percentile), resulting in a 4-month, 10-day age equivalent, while the Gross motor scale score was 3 (1st percentile; 4-month age level). The Motor Composite score was 64 (1st percentile: 57–71); this being extremely low (approximately at a 4–5-month age level and greater than 2 SDs below average).

Aaron's Adaptive Behavior score was 66 (extremely low; 1st percentile), with particular problems found in Communication (Communication Domain 59; 0.3 percentile; > 2 SDs below average), while Socialization was an area of relative strength (standard score 73; 4th percentile).

On the Social-Emotional scale, Aaron's scaled score of 2 was at the 2nd percentile; his sensory score was indicative of possible challenges due primarily to underreactivity. The youngster's Social-Emotional score was 60 (0.4 percentile; ± 2). This score falls in the extremely low range.

Level II

There was uniformity with regard to subtest scale scores with the exception of the Cognitive scale that fell in the low average range. However, items at this age tap social interactions, habituation, and sensorimotor function. The nature of these items could possibly cause inflation of scores, as could targeted early intervention efforts. All other scales fell in the extremely low range. ASD indicators were negative for items involving caregiver interactions on the Bayley-4 cognitive scale and the infant displayed a social smile and calmed when picked up—all contraindicative of early ASD behaviors. Most language-related ASD items were not passed, but this seemed to be due to developmental delays versus ASD per se. Due to Aaron's age and restricted behavioral repertoire, information gleaned from the ASD Checklist is limited.

Level III: (Synthesis and discussion)

Aaron is functioning in the extremely low range on most scales, the exception being the Cognitive Composite. This is addressed in Level II analyses, but the cognitive scale is an area of relative strength at this time that should be emphasized to the parents. Conversely, language is a major area of deficit. Noteworthy is the fact that language (particularly expressive) is a frequent area of weakness in children with DS and this worsens with increasing age. However, in Aaron's case, it would behoove his PCP to order a hearing test, given the magnitude of these delays, his erratic responses to sounds, and the tendency of children with DS to often have hearing deficits. As indicated previously, most children with Down Syndrome have scores that fall in the mild to moderate range of intellectual disability later on (i.e., 50–60), although the Cognitive composite score found during the current testing raises cautious optimism that the infant may show only mild deficits later, especially if a hearing impairment is found and corrected. Once again, serial testing would be in order, as would continuation with EI services. When discussing the findings with the parents, relative strengths in socialization and nonverbal cognitive abilities should be highlighted, but the clinician should also mention the fact that, in many children with Down Syndrome, overall scores tend to decrease over time due to the high frequency of language deficits. Aaron, however, will show us over time.

Case 3: Ralphie

Ralphie is a 21-month, 14-day-old infant born at 25 weeks gestational age, with a birth weight of 695 g. His age at time of assessment, corrected for prematurity, is 18–months. His perinatal history was complicated by a Grade IV intraventricular hemorrhage (periventricular hemorrhagic infarction) with greater involvement of the parenchyma on the right side, respiratory distress syndrome (RDS), bronchopulmonary dysplasia (BPD), hyperbilirubinemia, apnea/bradycardia, and retinopathy of prematurity (ROP) stage III, requiring laser surgery. He remained in the high-risk nursery for 109 days after birth.

Ralphie's parents had been reluctant to secure Early Intervention services, repeatedly saying that his development is not a concern. However, they became more alarmed when they compared him to a 22-month-old typically developing cousin at a recent family gathering. After this encounter, they reluctantly acknowledged that Ralphie's development might be a bit slow. Ralphie wears glasses. He was administered the Bayley-4 after being referred to a Children's Diagnostic Clinic by his PCP who identified motor concerns at 9 and 18 months, even though parent-report questionnaires were negative.

Findings: (Level I)

Ralphie received a Bayley-4 Cognitive scale score of 6 (9th percentile; borderline range). His Cognitive Composite Score was 80 (9th percentile, 95% CI 73–87; >1 SD below average), this falling in the low average to borderline range. Ralphie's cognitive score was at a 13-month-age level and reflects a 5-month delay (28%).

Ralphie obtained a Receptive Communication scaled score of 8 (25th percentile; low average); his Expressive Communication scale score was 5 (5th percentile; extremely low). Receptive skills were at a 15-month age level, while Expressive abilities were at an 11-month age equivalent. Therefore, receptive language was delayed by 3 months (17%) and expressive communication skills by 7 months (39%). The toddler's Language Composite was 79 (8th percentile; ±7; > 1 SD below average), this falling in the borderline range.

Ralphie's Fine Motor scale score was 5 (5th percentile; extremely low); his Gross Motor scale score was 4 (2nd percentile; extremely low). Ralphie's Motor Composite score was 69 (2nd percentile; 62–76). This score also falls in the extremely low range. Both the fine and gross motor scores were at an 11 month age equivalent, indicating a 39% delay in motor function (>2 SDs below average).

The youngster's Adaptive Composite score was 79 (8th percentile; ±4), this being in the borderline range. The Communication domain was the main area of deficit (66; ±5).

The Social/Emotional score was 75 (5th percentile). Some sensory processing items such as hyperreactivity to sounds and body movement issues were noted, but the overall score did not fall in the "possible challenges" category.

Level II

There was a statistically significant difference between the Receptive Communication and Gross Motor scale scores (0.05 level). The youngster has not received the diagnosis of CP at this time, although this diagnosis is still a possibility subsequently. A fair number of items on the ASD Checklist were endorsed, but Ralphie was social, and it seemed that many indicators were due to sensory issues and developmental problems.

Level III: (Synthesis and discussion)

Ralphie's receptive communication skills are in the low average range, while his Cognitive, Adaptive, and Social/Emotional scores are borderline. Motor skills are extremely low as are expressive communication abilities. These findings suggest that Ralphie may have strengths that cannot be tapped at this time due to motor issues. His expressive communication abilities differ from receptive skills by a standard deviation and it is possible that motor issues also have a negative impact on verbal production and articulation.

When attempting to run, the youngster stumbles, has a wide-based gait, tends to drag his left leg, and posture his left arm so that it does not swing in rhythm with his legs. These observations are compatible with spastic diplegia, which often is a sequela of PVH with more damage to the parenchyma of the right side (although this diagnosis should be made by a developmental/behavioral pediatrician or a pediatric neurologist). The youngster's fine motor skills could be affected by the ROP and his need for glasses, particularly since up to 75% of infants born EPT have visual perceptual and visual motor integrative issues. Motor tracts in the brain are in the area most typically affected by damage caused by PVH. Moreover, motor function is more directly affected by medical/biological influences than are other domains.

Feedback might be more difficult, given the parents' previous behaviors. Techniques gleaned from Chapter 14 would prove helpful, starting off with asking them what they perceive to be Ralphie's areas of strengths and also what domains are most concerning. Devising a plan for intervention that would include OT/PT, S/L, and referral to other subspecialists would be a good start, with a 6-month follow-up appointment set up as well. Note that motor skills tend to improve somewhat over time, in contrast to cognitive or significant language deficits.

Case 4: Paige

Paige is a 32-month, 12-day-old female who appears to have language delays. The delays are suspected to be in both Receptive and Expressive language domains. She was born full-term and without complications. Prenatal care was inconsistent. There are concerns with Paige's articulation (intelligibility) as well. She rarely produces two-word sentences and intelligibility (unfamiliar adults being able to understand what she says) is approximately 25% at best. According to her mother, Paige for "a long time" used to only say the first part of words (e.g., "ca" for cake, "ba" for ball, etc.). Motor skills are reportedly in the average range. Paige lives with her mother and maternal grandmother. The family is on public assistance and reside in subsidized housing, with Paige being covered by Medicaid. Her mom works part-time in a fast-food establishment. Paige did not receive Early Intervention services, but the family is planning to have her enroll in Head Start.

Findings: (Level I)

Paige received a Bayley-4 Cognitive Composite score of 95 (37th percentile; 95% CI 88–102). This falls in the average range and is at a 28-month age equivalent. The discrepancy between Paige's chronological age and her cognitive age equivalent is 4-months, which is of minimal significance (12% delay).

The youngster's Receptive Communication scale score was 7 (16th percentile: borderline), while her Expressive Communication scale score was 5 (5th percentile; very low). Her receptive and expressive age equivalents were 21 months and 19 months, respectively. Receptively, she was 11 months below her chronologic age (34% delay), and expressively, 13 months (41%). Paige's Language Composite score was 77 (6th percentile; 95% CI 70–84). This score is in the borderline range (and is approximately 1.5 SDs below average).

With respect to motor skills, Paige obtained a Fine Motor scale score of 11 (63rd percentile; average) and a Gross Motor scale score of 11 as well. Her Motor Composite score was 106 (66th percentile; 99–113). Fine motor skills were at a 34-month age level, while Gross motor abilities were at a 35-month age equivalent. Neither score indicated a delay.

Paige's Bayley-4 Adaptive Behavior Composite score was 89 (23rd percentile), this falling in the low average range. As would be expected from the previous test findings, the Communication Domain was the lowest adaptive score on the Bayley-4 (70; 2nd percentile; 2 SDs below average). Daily living and Social scores were in the average range (91 and 94, respectively). The ASD Checklist was unremarkable. The Social/Emotional Questionnaire was not given.

Level II

The Receptive and Expressive Communication scale scores differed significantly from the cognitive and motor scores. Language function ranged from a 19- to a 21-month age equivalent. Motor skills were average as were nonverbal cognitive abilities. Adaptive Communication skills were comparable to Bayley-4 Expressive and Receptive Communication subscales.

Level III: (Synthesis and discussion)

Paige currently displays characteristics of a developmental language delay. The possibility of specific language disorder is high, given her history, difficulty producing sentences, not understanding directions, poor intelligibility of verbal productions, and the fact that cognitive skills are an area of strength. It is possible that environmental factors place her language development at risk, but the qualitative observations of the young lady's language suggest this could not account for the entire problem.

Paige would benefit from EI speech and language services immediately and plans to have her enrolled in an Early Childhood Education program when she turns 3 years of age should be pursued now. She would also benefit from a hearing evaluation, particularly given her past history of only saying the first syllable of words.

CHAPTER 14
Providing feedback

Contents

A prime reason for assessment with the Bayley-4 is to identify children whose development is problematic. Because the infant or toddler was most likely referred for this reason, logically there is a greater likelihood of finding developmental delays than in the general population (i.e., there is a higher base rate). Typically, examiners who administered the Bayley-4 explain test results to caregivers or other professionals. Unfortunately, these results frequently involve "bad news" and often confirm the parents' fears that their child is not "normal."

Providing caregivers with such news is stressful for examiners, but it is important that findings be provided in an appropriate fashion. Withholding or censoring bad news in order to "protect" the family (the underlying assumption being what the family doesn't know won't hurt them) should not occur. Most clinicians have little or no formal training in providing feedback and have acquired skills in this area by experience. Many feel underprepared and do not have a plan or strategy for engaging in this activity (Novak, Morgan, McNamara, & te Velde, 2019). Feedback involves review of scores, discussion of performance on structured tasks, observations of spontaneous behaviors, interpretation of what the scores mean, identification of strengths, observation of verbal and nonverbal clues, and addressing questions posed by parents (Aylward, 1994). The examiner also needs to "read the process" in real time, meaning that it is necessary to be sensitive and able to detect subtle changes in the caregivers' effect during the

Bayley 4 Clinical Use and Interpretation
https://doi.org/10.1016/B978-0-12-817754-9.00014-3

meeting. At the risk of sounding dogmatic, this is not a session where scores are simply rattled off in rapid succession, thoroughly confusing and overwhelming caregivers; instead, it should involve a reciprocal dialogue where the examiner must also listen and be supportive of the child's family.

Initiation of feedback

It is helpful for clinicians to anticipate what difficult questions may be raised and develop potential answers ahead of time (Novak et al., 2019). At the outset, the clinician is advised to ask the parents about their thoughts regarding the developmental status of their child, concerns they might have, what they've been told thus far, and how they would compare their child's levels of development (e.g., cognitive, motor, language) to other children of the same age. The general rule is "ask before you tell." Since the caregivers most likely were present during testing, they may be familiar with some of the test tasks and behaviors that underlie the points being made—these provide concrete examples and "grounding." Caretakers also most likely provided caregiver feedback to questions posed by the examiner during testing. The examiner should also identify test behaviors that were indicative of strengths and ask what things the child does especially well. This procedure will help gauge how best to present the current findings and the likelihood of caregivers' acceptance of these findings (Aylward, 1994).

Parents sometimes challenge the Bayley-4 findings when their view of their child's development differs from the level indicated by the standardized, norm-referenced data. This potential conflict could be exacerbated further by the fact that even though "hard data" have been collected, the caregivers perceive that clinical judgments and potential bias are still involved. When there is disagreement, emotions intensify and this may decrease the caregiver's receptivity to what the examiner is saying (Pragatano & Gray, 2011). Every effort should be made by the clinician to not take disagreements personally.

The elephant in the room is the elusive prognosis. Caregivers want honest information about their child's future. Unfortunately, this is particularly difficult with regard to development because of the uncertainty in terms of underlying brain disruption or insult, recovery, effects of the environment, and relatively poor long-term predictability from infant tests in general. A careful balance needs to be developed between minimizing findings and causing excessive alarm. In most cases, the examiner can inform the parents that there is a high degree of certainty that the infant will make developmental progress, but the rate and ultimate level of developmental outcome is more elusive and cannot be predicted.

Tools to facilitate feedback

Use of a graphic such as the one depicted in Fig. 14.1 is helpful in such discussions. The mean score should be considered the "average" score (use of "normal" score immediately makes a child with lower scores "abnormal"); parents are more accepting when presented with the terms "below average," "emerging", or "borderline" than with "not normal." When using the graph, one should discuss how 50% of the population score below the mean, while 50% score above. Composite scores could be plotted on the *x*-axis of the curve so that the caregivers can understand visually where their child falls in each area. The Bayley-4 *Caregiver Report* form is extremely helpful in the feedback session and should be utilized routinely. Page 3 of the form enables the examiner to graphically illustrate the child's performance on the subscales for comparative purposes. The blank space on page 7 and the back cover can be used for note-taking or further graphic illustrations. Use of percentile ranks is also helpful in reflecting how the child does in relation to peers. For example, if the infant received a Cognitive Composite score of 85, this would fall at approximately the 16th percentile, indicating that roughly 84% of infants do better than the child being evaluated. In general, standard scores should be used as these are more precise—much more so than age equivalents. Caregivers may benefit from being given a copy of the normal

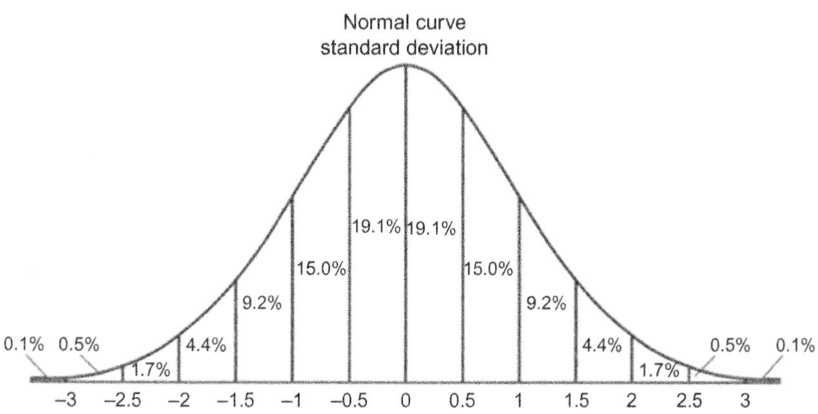

Fig. 14.1 The normal distribution (bell-shaped curve).

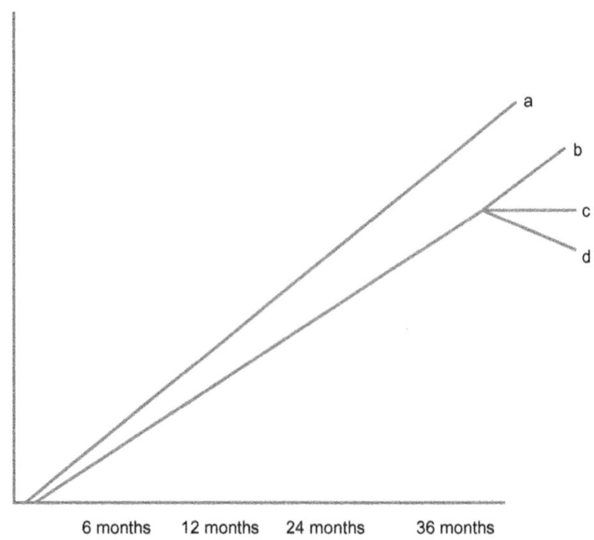

Fig. 14.2 Hypothetical diagram to explain developmental trajectory.

distribution figure as well as the Bayley-4 Caregiver Report (that also includes general intervention strategies; pp. 4–7). It is recommended that the caregivers be given a written report so that they can review what had been discussed and share it with other family members and professionals.

The infant's rate of development can be explained using Fig. 14.2. Line A represents the "average" developmental slope over time. In this example, at 12 months, a hypothetical infant's developmental slope (line B) is below average. The three lines (B, C, and D) represent possible future developmental progressions. Suggesting that the child's developmental level would fall somewhere between A and B is reasonable, although the caregiver would prefer that their child's slope will be closer to A. It is advisable for the examiner to not offer false hope in that regard by indicating that the likelihood is not high that the child would move up to the trajectory delineated by A, particularly if there is a major discrepancy between the slopes. It could be mentioned that lines C and D at 36+ months are a possibility, but also are not likely. Feedback should be presented in as the child "will tell us over time" and that the examiner would be delighted to have the child do better than expected. It is helpful to underscore that the child will make progress over time—how much and how fast are the two unknowns.

Feedback is easier when the child's slope is only several months below the typical one. Unlike the first scenario, here it becomes more difficult to discriminate a deficit from a delay, as well as prognosticate how the child will progress in the future. There is more reason for optimism and a greater possibility of a delay, versus a deficit, and these concepts should be discussed with the caretaker(s). Referring to Fig. 14.2, the child's developmental slope may be closer to line A, and this should suggest a greater likelihood of improvement. It should also be emphasized that the current evaluation provides a snapshot of the child and serial evaluation will be necessary to obtain a more valid estimate of the infant's development. Incidentally, this is one of the criticisms brought up by proponents of authentic assessment (e.g., Bagnato, Neisworth, & Pretti-Frontczak, 2010) who endorse continuous assessment and monitoring. Clinicians who use standardized norm-referenced assessment tools such as the Bayley-4 should also be aware that assessment of infants and children sometimes is a contentious issue with distinctions being drawn between the terms "testing" versus "assessment."

Examiners must exercise caution that they do not provide euphemisms for a problematic developmental finding in an effort to not alarm the caregivers. Global Developmental Delay (GDD) could be such a euphemism for a young child who shows developmental problems in two or more areas, and the degree of problems is major (e.g., the Bayley-4 Cognitive and Language Composites are both < 70). There is a good chance that this toddler may subsequently be diagnosed with an Intellectual Disability (ID). GDD should be considered a temporary diagnosis or placeholder for possible ID and should be framed as such. In general, practitioners want to avoid stressful interactions with the family when discussing the potential stigma of a "disability." This may be helpful in the short term, but when ID or a significant disability later becomes a reality, the parents will resent the practitioner for "not being honest" with them at the outset and for giving them false hope. In many ways, this is analogous to passengers who hear their plane is delayed, but still presume that it eventually will arrive, versus it actually has been canceled (Cohen & Houtrow, 2019).

Age equivalents/percent delay

Age equivalents are used frequently in developmental assessment and make the most sense to caregivers. They are also used in computation of percent delay. However, these are gross estimates that are often inaccurate. Age equivalents refer to the age at which a child's raw score is comparable to standardized age norms that are considered "average" for a given age. For example, consider a 12-month-old infant who is functioning at a 6-month age level on the Bayley-4 Cognitive Composite. Parents may assume that the 6-month delay is static or fixed; in so doing they might anticipate that the child would be functioning at approximately an 18-month level at the chronological age of 24 months, or at a 36-month level when he is 42 months of age. The concept of a "ratio" or proportion should be explored with the caregivers, indicating that 6 months/12 months approximate a 50% delay and that, at 24 months, there is a good chance that the toddler will be functioning closer to a 12-month level than at an 18-month age equivalent, again emphasizing the psychometric weakness of the age equivalent concept.

Related to age equivalents is the issue of "percent delay." In a similar fashion, this metric (term used loosely) is heavily dependent on the measurement (test) that is used for the numerator. A 6-month old who is functioning at a 3-month level has a 50% delay. However, a 24-month old toddler functioning at a 12-month level also has a 50% delay, as would a 36-month old child who functions at an 18-month age level. The differences between the developmental ages (estimated by the test given) are 3, 12, and 18 months. These differences add to the impreciseness of the developmental results and argue for use of standard deviations or z-scores.

Continuum of concerns

When discussing developmental outcomes, a modification of the AAP's DSM-PC (Wolraich, Felice, & Drotar, 1996) concept of a continuum of developmental concerns is useful; namely, whether a given developmental finding is: (1) a normal developmental variation; (2) a problem; or (3) a disorder—depending on degree and area of delay. A *Variation* can be considered a mild delay that should improve over time (e.g., a Motor Composite score of 85 without evidence of CP or a DCD, given that motor function has a self-righting tendency). A *Problem* is more concerning and is indicative of a significant delay in an area that feasibly could improve over time without intervention, although intervention may indeed be helpful (e.g., a Cognitive Composite score of 80). A *Disorder* is more severe in terms of presentation (e.g., CP; Bayley-4 Cognitive Composite of <70) and will require more intensive intervention that may or may not produce substantial change. Using this hypothetical continuum often clarifies the current evaluation findings for the parents.

Again, depending on the area and degree of the deficit, it is helpful to forewarn caregivers about terms they may encounter from other professionals over the course of the infant and child's development such as global developmental delay, cerebral palsy, intellectual disability, or a developmental coordination disorder. Even if no obvious major deficits are discerned on the Bayley-4, but the child is a member of a specific risk group (e.g., children born EPT), the parents should be cautioned that there still is the possibility of later high prevalence, low severity dysfunctions such as learning disabilities, ADHD, or executive dysfunction (Aylward, 2002, 2005). Examiners should refrain from "labeling" an infant or toddler; use of "developmental delay" is adequate early on. There is a series of hurdles parents of children with suspected developmental delays face. The first is viability (usually resolved by the time the family encounters the examiner); second is the presence of major disabilities (e.g., CP, severe developmental delay); third is minor disabilities (high prevalence/low severity dysfunctions); fourth is social and academic functioning; and lastly is future success in employment and relationships. With each successive concern, the examiner's ability to answer the question becomes more tentative or speculative. On the Bayley-4, major disabilities can be ruled out, but other concerns cannot be answered until the child is older.

Application of results

One of the most critical components of feedback involves development of a plan to address the delay(s) identified on the Bayley-4. Parents want to do something to help their child and they are empowered if a game plan is developed. Although "any plan is better than no plan" (R.E. Merrill, personal communication many years ago), a realistic plan is necessary. Bagnato et al. (2010) underscore the fact that assessment must be linked to intervention. In this approach, assessment results are used to address the identified problem(s). It also involves collaboration of both caregivers and professionals in order to maximize the child's potential. Planning for early intervention in the form of physical, occupational, developmental, and/or speech/language services, enrollment in an Early Childhood Education setting, or referring for more specific diagnostic or treatment services by specialists in pediatric neurology, genetics, ophthalmology, or orthopedics are examples of "doing something" about the developmental concerns.

When the examiner provides feedback to the child's primary care physician, more technical concepts can be used such as 95% confidence intervals, sensitivity and specificity concerns, what ratio developmental quotients really mean, and the reasoning underlying recommendations for interventions and/or referrals.

Positive attributes of the infant should be underscored regardless of degree of impairment. Rather than using terms such as weakness or deficit, it is recommended that these terms be realistically reframed as "areas where we want to see improvement," "areas not developed yet," or "areas of emerging skills." Each child is a unique individual, has a "personality," and it is advantageous to acknowledge these attributes. Even in cases of severe impairment, examiners still can make positive comments such as how pretty the baby's eyes are, what a nice bow in her hair, how social he is, what she does well, or how he is tuned in and attached to the caregiver. The child is more like peers than not like them. If a toddler has not performed well during testing, an easy item or two could be presented toward the end of the session, so the parent can see the child being successful.

Determining if the message got through

It is helpful for the examiner to have the parents indicate the "take home" messages of the feedback session. This is facilitated by saying, "I just want to make sure that I had told you the important information, because sometimes I may get sidetracked and overlook something or not get my point across." Presented in this manner, the responsibility for miscommunication is placed on the examiner and the parents will not feel they are being spoken down to or criticized. Parents routinely will want to know *why* their child is delayed. When dealing with established risk (e.g., Down syndrome, Fragile X, Rhett syndrome), the causes are identifiable. With biological risk (e.g., being born EPT), although the probability of risk increases, the specific etiology of the delay may not be as clear. With respect to environmental risk, care must be taken so as not to make it seem that it is the caregivers' fault. Furthermore, the specific cause for a developmental delay simply cannot be identified in a high percentage of children.

Caregivers often receive well-intentioned but incorrect advice from friends or family members. This "advice" can be dismissive or minimizing ("he'll catch up"; "his uncle did the same thing when he was younger but he's okay now"), or the comments can be more critical ("I told you there's something wrong with his language"; "when are you going to get her walking checked out?"; or "she acts autistic"). Asking about these misguided sources of stress and identifying how family, friends, or caregiver groups can provide support is recommended. Parents should be cautioned about doing "research" on the internet; it is helpful for clinicians to have a listing of internet sites that can be given to the parents. Evidence-based treatments should be included.

The examiner's overall goal should be to identify main findings to present and repeat these during the dialogue. Too much information can be overwhelming. The "5C's" are recommended when engaging in feedback: be clear, concise, correct (accurate), comforting, and corrective (helpful) (Pragatano & Gray, 2011).

Correction for prematurity

Many parents of infants born preterm will raise the question whether their child will catch up to peers. The answer depends on several factors: the specific outcome that is under consideration, the child's pre-, peri-, and postnatal medical course, and the degree of prematurity. Some investigators argue that children born preterm may never totally catch up—rather, differences between those born prematurely and their peers simply become less obvious over time (Doyle & Anderson, 2016).

Correction, which has been utilized since the 1930s (Wilson & Cradock, 2004), is controversial. Correction is based on a biological perspective in which there is predetermined maturation of the CNS; it is thought to decrease transient delay until there is ample time for the preterm infants to catch up to full-term peers. The use of chronologic age places more emphasis on environmental factors such as stimulation and medical care (Wilson & Cradock, 2004). Correction for prematurity involves subtracting the number of weeks that the infant was born prematurely from the child's chronological age to arrive at the corrected age (D'Agostino, 2009). Take, for example, a child born at 28-week gestation who is being tested at 9 months chronologic age. She is 3-month premature and therefore is 6 months corrected age.

There are multiple issues that cause correction to be a conundrum. These include: (1) whether correction should be used at all; (2) should correction be applied to all domains of development (Morsan, Fantoni, & Tallandini, 2018); (3) up to what age should correction be applied; (4) should correction be restricted to certain gestational ages at birth (e.g., those born EPT and VPT, but not MPT or LPT; Parekh et al., 2016); and (5) should partial correction be considered?

Correcting for prematurity or age adjustment could actually result in a lower score because the Bayley-4 start point would be lower and the child would not automatically receive credit for items preceding the start point (Parekh et al., 2016). This was a particular problem with the Bayley-II.

There is general agreement that some correction is needed when children who were born preterm are assessed, and this should be explained to parents and caregivers. Correction up to 2 years is the most popular convention and is underscored in the Bayley-4 manual, although correction to 3 years has also been endorsed (Wilson-Ching, Pascoe, Doyle, & Anderson, 2014), particularly in children born EPT. Some researchers recommend correction as late as early childhood (van Veen, Aarnoudse-Moens, van Kaam, Oosterlaan, & van Wassenaer-Leemhuis, 2016), while others suggest stopping at 12 or 24 months (Morsan et al., 2018; Restiffe & Gherpelli, 2005).

More recently, the Bayley-4 Cognitive, Language, and Motor scales were subject to analyses similar to those employed by Wilson Ching et al. (Aylward, 2019). In the cognitive realm, correction is necessary during the first 2 years and also appears warranted at 3 years in those children born 4 months premature (24 weeks of gestation). Language and Motor function needs to be corrected to 3 years for all gestational ages. Hence, these data suggest that the degree of maturity at birth is an important determining factor on how long correction may need to be applied (Doyle & Anderson, 2016).

At later ages, there still is some effect, particularly because of the application of 3-month age bands on the Bayley from 36 months onwards (Veldhuizen, Rodriguez, Wade, & Cairney, 2015) or on later intelligence tests (van Veen et al., 2016). What this means is that if the uncorrected age was at the beginning of a 3-month normative age band, the child would be at more disadvantage than if the uncorrected age fell toward the end (upper limit) of the age band. Roberts et al. (2013) reported a 1/3 standard deviation difference in WPPSI-III corrected and uncorrected scores at age 5, and less than a two-point difference at age 8, again suggesting that differences exist but become less discernable at later ages.

There are other practical ramifications as well. If a child was born EPT, the uncorrected age may make him or her eligible to enter kindergarten, while the corrected age would suggest that he or she may be better off waiting until the following year. Noteworthy is the trend for "academic redshirting" in many children born premature, where their parents start them in school a year later than they could qualify for (even by uncorrected age). At earlier ages (below 3 years), correction would reduce the number of children eligible for EI services; conversely, uncorrected scores would result in children being eligible for services they may not need.

We are left with the question of what to say to parents regarding correction for prematurity. First, what is said will depend on the child's gestational age at birth. Based on the Bayley-4 normative data, it is recommended that all scores (i.e., cognitive, motor, language) be corrected (Aylward, 2019). The 2-year convention, endorsed by the American Academy of Pediatrics (Bernbaum, Campbell, & Imaizumi, 2009), was initially selected for the Bayley-4 and this should be followed, although indicating corrected and uncorrected scores at later ages is recommended for EPT infants in particular.

CHAPTER 15

The Bayley-4 Screening Test

Contents

Description

A brief discussion of the Bayley-4 Screening Test is warranted in this final chapter (Bayley & Aylward, 2019c). This test contains a subset of Cognitive, Language, and Motor items drawn from the full Bayley-4 and provides a rapid, yet psychometrically sound, means of identifying children who are at risk for developmental problems. The Bayley-4 Screening Test contains 30 Cognitive items, 22 Receptive Communication, 23 Expressive Communication, 27 Fine Motor, and 27 Gross Motor items.

Items tap the major functions for each domain as indicated in Chapters 3 through 7. It is not necessary to administer all five screening subtests, although doing so is strongly recommended because this would provide a broader overall screening, yet still not require a large amount of time. Item administration and scoring criteria are the same as those found in the full Bayley-4. On a cautionary note, a diagnosis cannot be made based on screening test data, but instead the data can be used to identify areas of function that warrant further evaluation with the full Bayley-4 or a pediatric subspecialist.

Age groupings

Normative data age groups for the screening test differ a bit from the Bayley-4; this is done to make age determination easier (e.g., 10 through

Bayley 4 Clinical Use and Interpretation
https://doi.org/10.1016/B978-0-12-817754-9.00015-5

13 months, 21 through 24 months, etc.). Correction for prematurity is recommended at least through age 2 years. These age groupings are as follows:

- 16 days–3 months:30 days
- 4.0 months to 6 months 30 days
- 7.0 months to 9 months 30 days
- 10.0–13:30
- 14.0–17:30
- 18.0–20:30
- 21.00–24:30
- 25.0–30:30
- 31.0–36:30
- 37.0–42:30

Scoring

Cut-score norms for the Bayley-4 Screening Test are used for the 10 age groups listed previously. The cut-offs group children into *High Risk* (0 to 2nd percentile), *Moderate Risk* (3rd to 25th percentile), and *Low Risk* (26th to 100th percentile) categories, based on the likelihood of developmental delay. Selection of items was based on percentiles in the normative sample, comparisons to specific clinical groups (e.g., cognitive compared to children with DS; Cognitive, Receptive, and Expressive Language to those with Language Delay, Fine and Gross Motor performance to children with Motor Impairment, etc.), consideration of item face validity, and the ability to measure skills deemed important developmentally. Item selection also was influenced by the goal of limiting the number of test materials required for administration.

Similar to the full Bayley-4, there are reversal and discontinue rules. The child must receive a score of 2 on the first item presented at the age-specific start point in order to proceed. If a 1 or 0 score is obtained, the item at the start point of the previous age for that subtest is then administered (basal). Four consecutive scores of 0 determine the criterion for discontinuation (ceiling). There are only four start points included. Using the first start point as an example, the first seven items on the Cognitive scale are probably too easy for a 6-month old and can be skipped, provided the infant receives a score of 2 on the first item that is then administered. Similarly, a 13-month old would be too advanced for the first four items on start point B. The items do rapidly increase in difficulty, however.

Application

The Bayley-4 Screening Test can be employed to quickly evaluate the probability of risk for developmental delay in children seen individually by the practitioner. Typically, the child's physician, parents, or daycare provider may raise concerns about the child's development in comparison to same-aged peers. Since this one-on-one test is not routinely administered to all children but rather to those whose development is suspected, this is called targeted screening. However, groups of children can also be given the screener, but it still must be administered one-on-one. The screening test can be administered by EI specialists, physicians, psychologists, and pediatric rehabilitation professionals (OT, PT, S/L). If the child falls into the high-risk range on any developmental domain, further testing with the full Bayley-4 is warranted. If the infant or toddler scores in the borderline range in any area, close monitoring is prudent with follow-up screening given in several months. In the scenario where borderline scores are found in two or more areas, there are several options: (1) the screening test could be readministered in 2–3 months; (2) the specific areas in which the borderline scores were obtained could be administered from the Bayley-4; or (3) the full Bayley-4 can be given shortly after the initial screening (depending on the child's age and other clinical and medical findings). These procedures allow close developmental monitoring and the opportunity for early implementation of interventions.

A combination of the Bayley-4 Screening Test and the full Bayley-4 can be folded into longitudinal follow-up programs or research endeavors, when repeated serial administration of the full Bayley is not feasible due to cost, volume of children seen, or a limited number of examiners. For example, assume that children in an NICU high-risk follow-up program are seen at 6-, 12-, 24-, and 36-months (age corrected for prematurity). The screening test could be used at 6 and 24 months, while the full Bayley is given at 12 and 36 months. Obviously, there are other combinations that could be used employing the two tests.

Because this is a screening test, the goal is to identify as many at-risk children as possible. As a result, emphasis is placed on sensitivity. Applying this principle may identify children on the screening test as high-risk who actually are not (false-positives). Although this is an issue, incorrectly categorizing a child who has true delays as not being at risk (false-negatives) is much more problematic. Approximately 10% of children considered "typical" will receive one at-risk score, which is congruent with the extant literature. Combining the high and borderline risk categories produces the best sensitivity, missing very few children who have delays, but because the borderline risk category includes children up to the 25th percentile, there is a greater likelihood of false-positives.

Classification accuracy

Psychometric data for the test are found in the Bayley-4 Screening Manual (Bayley & Aylward, 2019c); however, several points deserve mention. In comparing the classification accuracy of the screening test to the full Bayley-4, when the scaled scores for the Bayley-4 ranged from 1 to 4 (≤2nd percentile), the percentage of high-risk screening test scores ranged from 54% (Cognitive) to 67% (Gross Motor). When the Bayley-4 scaled scores ranged from 5 to 7 (3rd to 25th percentile), the percentage of children falling in the borderline risk category on the screener ranged from 71% (Gross Motor) to 87% (Expressive Communication). Bayley-4 scale scores of 8 and above corresponded to low-risk screening test scores in 79% (Receptive communication) to 84% (Cognitive) of children (Bayley & Aylward, 2019c).

Similarly, the normative sample was compared to the aforementioned clinical groups in terms of number of high-risk classifications. These could range from any 1 scale to all 5 scales being high-risk. As indicated earlier, 9.6% of the children in the normative group had any 1 score falling into the high-risk category, while the clinical groups ranged from 24% to 91%. When the criterion of any 2 scores being high-risk was evaluated, only 3.3% of the normative sample but 8%–91% of the clinical groups had any 2 scores in the high-risk range (the clinical group with the lowest percentage was children with language delay). Less than 2% of the normative sample had ≥3 high-risk scores, while as much as 52% of the clinical had 3, 42% 4, and 19% had all 5 scores in the high-risk range.

Summary

These data indicate good congruence between the Bayley-4 and the Bayley-4 Screening Test. To reiterate, as a general recommendation, if 1 or more domains fall in the high-risk range on the screener, the full Bayley should be administered, even though close to 10% of "normals" receive this risk rating. This may be due to the possibility that some of the children in the normative sample had unidentified developmental issues. If 1 scale falls in the borderline risk range, rescreening in 2–3 months should be implemented. In the scenario where 2 or more scales fall into the borderline range, the examiner has three options: rescreen in 2–3 months, administer the corresponding Bayley-4 subscales for the areas producing the borderline scores (i.e., Cognitive, Language (RC and EC), or Motor (FM and GM)), or administer the entire Bayley-4 shortly after the initial screening.

References

Accardo, P. J., Accardo, J., & Capute, A. J. (2008). A neurodevelopmental perspective on the continuum of developmental disabilities. In P. J. Accardo (Ed.), *Capute and Accardo's neurodevelopmental disabilities in infancy and childhood* (3rd ed., pp. 3–23). Baltimore, MD: Paul H. Brookes.

Adams-Chapman, I., Heyne, R. J., De Mauro, S. B., Duncan, A. F., et al. (2018). Neurodevelopmental impairment among extremely preterm infants in the neonatal research network. *Pediatrics, 141*, 1–11.

Allison, C., Auyeung, B., & Baron-Cohen, S. (2012). Toward brief "red flags" for autism screening: The short autism Spectrum Quotient and the Short Quantitative Checklist in 1,000 cases and 3,000 controls. *Journal of the American Academy of Child and Adolescent Psychiatry, 51*, 202–212.

Allison, C., Baron-Cohen, S., Wheelright, S., Charman, T., et al. (2008). The Q-CHAT (Quantitative Checklist for Autism in Toddlers): A normally distributed quantitative measure of autistic traits at 18-24 months of age: Preliminary report. *Journal of Autism and Developmental Disorders, 38*, 1414–1425.

American Academy of Pediatrics. (2006). Identifying infants and young children with developmental disorders in the medical home: An algorithm for developmental surveillance and screening. *Pediatrics, 118*, 405–420.

American Association on Intellectual and Developmental Disabilities (AAIDD). (2010). *Intellectual disability: Definition, classification and systems of support* (11th ed.). Washington, DC: AAIDD.

American Psychiatric Association. (2013). *Diagnostic and statistical manual of mental disorders* (5th ed.). Arlington, VA: American Psychiatric Association.

Amiel-Tison, C., & Gosselin, J. (2008). The Amiel-Tison and Gosselin neurological assessment from birth to 6 years of age. In P. J. Accardo (Ed.), *Capute and Accardo's neurodevelopmental disabilities in infancy and childhood* (3rd ed., pp. 321–333). Baltimore, MD: Paul A. Brookes Publishing.

Anderson, M. L. (2010). Neural reuse: A fundamental organizational principle of the brain. *Behavioral and Brain Sciences, 33*, 245–266.

Anderson, M. L. (2016). Neural reuse in the organization and development of the brain. *Developmental Medicine and Child Neurology, 58*(Suppl. 4), 3–6.

Anderson, P. J., De Luca, C. R., Hutchinson, E., Roberts, G., & Doyle, L. W. (2010). Underestimation of developmental delay by the new Bayley-III scale. *Archives of Pediatrics and Adolescent Medicine, 164*, 332–336.

Andrews, L., Davies, T. H., Linz, M., & Payne, M. (2018). Polydrug abuse and fetal exposure: A review. *Journal of Pediatrics and Child Health, 3*, 1–7.

Armstrong, K. H., & Agazzi, H. C. (2010). The Bayley III cognitive scale. In L. G. Weiss, T. Okland, & G. P. Aylward (Eds.), *Bayley-III clinical use and interpretation* (pp. 29–45). New York: Academic Press.

Aylward, G. P. (1988). Infant and early childhood assessment. In M. Tramontana & S. Hooper (Eds.), *Assessment issues in child neuropsychology* (pp. 225–248). New York: Plenum Press.

Aylward, G. P. (1992). The relationship between environmental risk and developmental outcome. *Journal of Developmental and Behavioral Pediatrics, 13*, 222–229.

Aylward, G. P. (1994). *Practitioner's guide to developmental and psychological testing*. New York: Plenum Publishing.

Aylward, G. P. (1995). *Bayley infant neurodevelopmental screener*. San Antonio, TX: The Psychological Corporation.

Aylward, G. P. (1997). *Infant and early childhood neuropsychology*. New York: Plenum Publishing Company.

Aylward, G. P. (2002). Cognitive and neuropsychological outcomes: More than IQ scores. *Mental Retardation and Developmental Disabilities Research Reviews, 8*, 234–240.

Aylward, G. P. (2005). Neurodevelopmental outcomes of infants born prematurely. *Journal of Developmental and Behavioral Pediatrics, 26*, 427–440.

Aylward, G. P. (2009). Developmental screening and assessment: What are we thinking? *Journal of Developmental and Behavioral Pediatrics, 30*, 169–173.

Aylward, G. P. (2010). Commentary. Environmental influences: Issues of timing and type. *Journal of Pediatric Psychology, 35*, 284–285.

Aylward, G. P. (2013). Continuing issues with the Bayley-III: Where do we go from here. *Journal of Developmental and Behavioral Pediatrics*, (9), 697–701.

Aylward, G. P. (2018). Issues in neurodevelopmental testing of infants born prematurely: The Bayley scales of infant development third edition and other tools. In H. Needelman & B. J. Jackson (Eds.), *Follow-up for NICU graduates. Promoting positive developmental and behavioral outcomes for at-risk infants* (pp. 241–253). New York: Springer.

Aylward, G. P. (2019). Is it correct to correct for prematurity? Theoretic analysis of the Bayley-4 normative data. *Journal of Developmental & Behavioral Pediatrics*, [in press].

Aylward, G. P., & Aylward, B. S. (2011). The changing yardstick in measurement of cognitive abilities in infancy. *Journal of Developmental and Behavioral Pediatrics, 32*, 465–468.

Aylward, G. P., & Verhulst, S. J. (2008). Comparison of caretaker report and hands-on screening in high-risk infants. *Developmental Neuropsychology, 33*, 124–136.

Aylward, G. P., & Zhu, J. J. (2019). *The Bayley Scales: Clarification for clinicians and researchers*. Technical Report (pp. 1–12). Bloomington, MN: NCS Pearson.

Bagnato, S. J., Neisworth, J. T., & Pretti-Frontczak, K. (2010). *LINKing authentic assessment & early childhood intervention* (2nd ed.). Baltimore, MD: Paul H. Brookes Publishing.

Baio, J., Wiggins, L., Christenson, D. L., et al. (2018). Prevalence of autism spectrum disorders among children aged 8 years—Autism and Developmental Disabilities Monitoring Network, 11 sites, United States, 2014. CDC *Morbidity and Mortality Weekly Report, 67*, 1–23.

Baird, H. W., & Gordon, E. C. (1983). Neurological evaluation of infants and children. *Clinics in developmental medicine, No. 84/85*. Philadelphia, PA: Lippincott.

Ball, G., Pazderova, L., Chew, A., Tusor, N., et al. (2015). Thalamocortical connectivity predicts cognition in children born preterm. *Cerebral Cortex, 25*, 4310–4318.

Bayley, N. (1969). *The Bayley scales of infant development*. New York: The Psychological Corporation.

Bayley, N. (1993). *The Bayley scales of infant development* (2nd ed.). San Antonio, TX: The Psychological Corporation.

Bayley, N. (2006). *Bayley scales of infant and toddler development* (3rd ed.). San Antonio, TX: The Psychological Corporation.

Bayley, N., & Aylward, G. P. (2019a). *Bayley scales of infant and toddler development* (4th ed.). Administration Manual. Bloomington, MN: NCS Pearson.

Bayley, N., & Aylward, G. P. (2019b). *Bayley scales of infant and toddler development* (4th ed.). Technical Manual. Bloomington, MN: NCS Pearson.

Bayley, N., & Aylward, G. P. (2019c). *Bayley scales of infant and toddler development* (4th ed.). Screening Test. Bloomington, MN: NCS Pearson.

Beck, D. M., Schaefer, C., Pang, K., & Carlson, S. M. (2011). Executive function in preschool children: Test-retest reliability. *Journal of Cognition and Development, 12*, 169–193.

Belsky, J. (2016). The differential susceptibility hypothesis. Sensitivity to the environment for better and for worse. *JAMA Pediatrics, 170*, 321–322.

Bernbaum, J. C., Campbell, D. E., & Imaizumi, S. O. (2009). Follow-up care of the graduate from the neonatal intensive care unit. In T. McInerny (Ed.), *American Academy of Pediatrics textbook of pediatric care* (pp. 867–882). Elk Grove Village, IL: American Academy of Pediatrics.

Bishop, D., Price, T., Dale, P., & Plomin, R. (2003). Outcomes of early language delay: Predicting persistent and transient language difficulties at 3 and 4 years. *Journal of Speech Language, and Hearing Research, 46*, 544–560.

Bishop, D.V., Snowling, M. J., Thompson, P. A., Greenhalgh, T., & CATALISE-2 Consortium. (2016). Phase 2 of CATALISE: A multinational and multidisciplinary Delphi consensus study of problems with language development: Identifying language impairments in children. *PLoS One, 11*, E0158753.

Bishop, D.V., Snowling, M. J., Thompson, P. A., Greenhalgh, T., & CATALISE-2 Consortium. (2017). Phase 2 of CATALISE: A multinational Delphi consensus study of problems with language development: Terminology. *Journal of Child Psychology and Psychiatry, 58*, 1068–1080.

Blaggan, S., Guy, A., Boyle, E. M., Spata, E., Manktelow, B. N., Wolke, D., et al. (2014). A parent questionnaire for developmental screening in infants born late and moderately preterm. *Pediatrics, 134*, e55–e62.

Blair, E. (2010). Epidemiology of the cerebral palsies. *Orthopedic Clinics of North America, 41*, 441–455.

Blair, C., & Raver, C. (2012). Child development in the context of adversity: Experiential canalization of brain and behavior. *American Psychologist, 67*, 309–318.

Blank, R., Barnett, A. L., Cairney, J., Green, D., et al. (2019). International clinical practice recommendations on the definition, diagnosis, assessment, intervention, and psychosocial aspects of developmental coordination disorder. *Developmental Medicine and Child Neurology, 61*, 242–285.

Bornstein, M. H., Hahns, C. S., Putnick, D. L., & Suwalsky, J. D. (2014). Stability of core language skills from early childhood to adolescence: A latent variable approach. *Child Development, 85*, 1346–1359.

Bowlby, R., & King, P. (2004). *Fifty years of attachment theory: Recollections of Donald Winnicott and John Bowlby*. London: Karnac Books.

Braun, K., & Bock, J. (2011). The experience-dependent maturation of prefronto-limbic circuits and the origin of developmental psychopathology: Implications for the pathogenesis and therapy of behavior disorders. *Developmental Medicine and Child Neurology, 53*(Suppl. 4), 14–19.

Brazelton, T. B., & Nugent, J. K. (2011). Neonatal behavioral assessment scale. *Clinics in developmental medicine, No. 190* (4th ed.). London: MacKeith Press.

Breinbauer, C., Mancil, T. L., & Greenspan, S. (2010). The Bayley-III social–emotional scale. In L. G. Weiss, T. Okland, & G. P. Aylward (Eds.), *Bayley-III clinical use and interpretation* (pp. 147–175). New York: Academic Press.

Bressler, S. L., & Menon, V. (2010). Large-scale brain networks in cognition: Emerging methods and principles. *Trends in Cognitive Sciences, 14*, 277–290.

Bricker, D., & Squires, J. (2009). *The ages and stages questionnaire* (3rd ed.). Baltimore, MD: Brookes Publishing.

Brito, N. H., Fifer, W. P., Amso, D., Barr, R., Bell, M. A., Calkins, S., et al. (2019). Beyond the Bayley: Neurocognitive assessments of development during infancy and toddlerhood. *Developmental Neuropsychology*, https://doi.org/10.1080/87565641.2018.1564310.

Brooks-Gunn, J., Duncan, G. J., & Aber, J. L. (1997). *Neighborhood poverty: Context and consequences for children*. New York: Russell Sage Foundation.

Brostrom, L., Vollmer, B., Bolk, J., Eklof, E., & Aden, U. (2018). Minor neurological dysfunction and associations with motor function, general cognitive abilities and behavior in children born extremely preterm. *Developmental Medicine and Child Neurology, 60*, 826–832.

Bush, S. S., Sweet, J. J., Bianchini, K. J., Johnson-Greene, D., Dean, P. M., & Schoenbery, M. R. (2018). Deciding to adopt revised and new psychological and neuropsychological tests: An inter-organizational position paper. *The Clinical Neuropsychologist, 32*, 319–325.

Campbell, C., & Shatz, C. J. (1992). Synapses formed by identified retinogeniculate axons during the segregation of eye input. *Journal of Neuroscience, 12*, 1847–1858.

Carlson, S. (2005). Developmentally sensitive measures of executive function in preschool children. *Developmental Neuropsychology, 28*, 573–594.

Case-Smith, J., & Alexander, H. (2010). The Bayley-III motor scale. In L. G. Weiss, T. Okland, & G. P. Aylward (Eds.), *Bayley-III clinical use and interpretation* (pp. 77–146). New York: Academic Press.

Casey, B. J., Giedd, J. N., & Thomas, K. M. (2000). Structural and functional brain development and its relation to cognitive development. *Biological Psychology, 54*, 241–257.

Champagne, F., & Curley, J. (2009). Epigenetic mechanisms mediating the long-term effects of maternal care on development. *Neuroscience and Biobehavioral Reviews, 33*, 593–600.

Chlebowski, C., Robins, D. L., Barton, M. L., & Fein, D. (2013). Large-scale use of the Modified Checklist for Autism in low risk toddlers. *Pediatrics, 131*, e1121–e1127.

Christian, E. A., Jin, D. L., Attenello, F., et al. (2016). Trends in hospitalization of preterm infants with intraventricular hemorrhage and hydrocephalus in United States, 2000-2010. *Journal of Neurosurgery: Pediatrics, 17*, 305–311.

Cohen, E., & Houtrow, A. (2019). Disability is not delay: Precision communication about intellectual disability. *Journal of Pediatrics, 207*, 241–243.

Crais, E. R. (2010). The Bayley-III language scale. In L. G. Weiss, T. Okland, & G. P. Aylward (Eds.), *Bayley-III clinical use and interpretation* (pp. 47–75). New York: Academic Press.

Cuevas, K., & Bell, M. A. (2014). Infant attention and early childhood executive function. *Child Development, 85*, 397–404.

D'Agostino, J. A. (2009). An evidentiary review regarding the use of chronological age and adjusted age in the assessment of preterm infants. *Journal for Specialists in Pediatric Nursing, 15*, 26–32.

Dale, P. S., Price, T. S., Bishop, D. S., & Plomin, R. (2003). Outcomes of early language delay: I. Predicting persistent and transient language difficulties at 3 and 4 years. *Journal of Speech Language and Hearing Research, 46*, 544–560.

Dan, B. (2017). The promise of epigenetics for neurodisability. *Developmental Medicine and Child Neurology, 59*, 238.

Dan, B. (2018). Very early diagnosis of autism spectrum disorder. *Developmental Medicine and Child Neurology, 60*, 1093–1100.

de Vries, A. M., & de Groot, L. (2002). Transient dystonias revisited: A comparative study of preterm and term children at 2 ½ years of age. *Developmental Medicine and Child Neurology, 44*, 415–421.

Diamond, A. (1990). The development and neural basis of memory functions as indexed by the AB and delayed response tasks in human infants and infant monkeys. *Annals of the New York Academy of Sciences, 608*, 267–309.

Diamond, A. (2000). Close interrelation of motor development and cognitive development and of the cerebellum and prefrontal cortex. *Child Development, 71*, 44–56.

Diamond, A. (2013). Executive functions. *Annual Review of Psychology, 64*, 135–165.

Dinstein, I., Pierce, K., Eyler, L., et al. (2011). Disrupted neural synchronization in toddlers with autism. *Neuron, 70*, 1218–1225.

Domellof, E., Johansson, A., & Ronnqvist, L. (2011). Handedness in preterm born children: A systematic review and meta-analysis. *Neuropsychologia, 49*, 2299–2310.

Domellof, E., Ronnqvist, L., Titram, M., Esseily, R., & Fagard, J. (2009). Atypical functional lateralization in children with fetal alcohol syndrome. *Developmental Psychobiology, 51*, 696–705.

Douglas-Escobar, M., & Weiss, M. D. (2015). Hypoxic-ischemic encephalopathy. A review for clinicians. *JAMA Pediatrics, 169*, 397–403.

Doyle, L. W., & Anderson, P. J. (2016). Do we need to correct age for prematurity when assessing children? *Journal of Pediatrics, 173*, 11–12.

Dykens, E. M., Hodapp, R. M., & Evans, D.W. (1994). Profiles and development of adaptive behavior in children with Down Syndrome. *American Journal of Mental Retardation, 98*, 580–587.

Ellis Weismer, S., & Evans, J. L. (2002). The role of processing limitations in early identification of specific language impairment. *Topics in Language Disorders, 22*, 15–29.

Espy, K. A., Stalets, M. M., McDiarmid, M. M., Senn, T. E., Cwik, M. F., & Hamby, A. (2002). Executive functions in preschool children born preterm: Application of cognitive neuroscience programs. *Child Neuropsychology, 8*, 83–92.

Feldman, H. M. (2019). How young children learn language and speech. *Pediatrics in Review, 40*, 398–410.

Fiori, S., & Guzzetta, A. (2015). Plasticity following early-life brain injury: Insights from quantitative MRI. *Seminars in Perinatology, 39*, 141–146.

Fu, M., & Zuo, Y. (2011). Experience-dependent structural plasticity in the cortex. *Trends in Neurosciences, 34*, 177–187.

Garon, N., Bryson, S. E., & Smith, I. M. (2006). Executive function in preschoolers: A review using an integrated framework. *Psychological Bulletin, 134*, 31–60.

Georgieff, M. K., Tran, P.V., & Carlson, E. S. (2018). Atypical fetal development: Fetal alcohol syndrome, nutritional deprivation, teratogens, and risk for neurodevelopmental disorders and psychopathology. *Development and Psychopathology, 30*, 1063–1086.

Gesell, A. (1945). *The embryology of behavior*. New York: Harper and Row.

Gilles, F., Gressens, P., Dammann, O., & Leviton, A. (2017). Hypoxia-ischemia is not an antecedent of most preterm brain damage: The illusion of validity. *Developmental Medicine and Child Neurology, 59*, 1–5.

Glascoe, F. P. (1998). *Collaborating with parents: Using parents' evaluation of developmental status to detect and address developmental and behavioral problems*. Nashville, TN: Ellsworth & Vandemeer Press.

Goldstein, M. H., & Schwade, J. A. (2008). Social feedback to infants' babbling facilitates rapid phonological learning. *Psychological Science, 19*, 515–523.

Goo, M., Tucker, K., & Johnston, L. M. (2018). Muscle tone assessments for children aged 0 to 12 years: A systematic review. *Developmental Medicine and Child Neurology, 60*, 660–671.

Greenough, W. T., Black, J. E., & Wallace, C. S. (1987). Experience and brain development. *Child Development, 58*, 539–559.

Greenough, W. T., & Chang, F. F. (1989). Plasticity of synapse structure and pattern in the cerebral cortex. In A. Peters & E. G. Jones (Eds.), *Vol. 7. Cerebral cortex* (pp. 391–440). New York: Plenum Press.

Greenspan, S. I. (1989). *The development of the ego: Implications for personality theory, psychopathology and the psychotherapeutic process*. Madison, CT: International Universities Press.

Greenspan, S. I. (1997). *The growth of the mind and the endangered origins of intelligence*. Cambridge, MA: Perseus Books.

Greenspan, S. I. (2004). *Greenspan social-emotional growth chart manual*. San Antonio, TX: Pearson.

Greenspan, S. I., & Shanker, S. (2004). *The first idea: How symbols, language and intelligence evolved from our primate ancestors to modern humans*. Cambridge, MA: Da Capo Press.

Greenspan, S. I., DeGangi, G. A., & Wieder, S. (2001). *The functional emotional assessment scale (FEAS) for infancy and early childhood: Clinical and research applications*. Bethesda, MD: Interdisciplinary Council on Developmental and Learning Disorders.

Guyer, A. E., Perez-Edgar, K., & Crone, E. A. (2018). Opportunities for neurodevelopmental plasticity from infancy through early adulthood. *Child Development, 98*, 687–697.

Haataja, L., Mercuri, E., Regev, R., Cowan, F., et al. (1999). Optimality score for the neurologic examination of the infant at 12 and 18 months of age. *Journal of Pediatrics, 135*, 153–160.

Hack, M., Taylor, H. G., Drotar, D., et al. (2005). Poor predictive validity of the Bayley Scales of Infant Development for cognitive function of extremely low birth weight children at school age. *Pediatrics, 116*, 333–341.

Hadders-Algra, M. (2002). Two distinct forms of minor neurological dysfunction. Perspectives emerging from of review of data of the Groningen Perinatal Project. *Developmental Medicine and Child Neurology, 44*, 561–571.

Hamer, E. G., & Hadders-Algra, M. (2016). Prognostic significance of neurological signs in high-risk infants-a systematic review. *Developmental Medicine and Child Neurology, 58*(Suppl. 4), 53–60.

Hardy, S., Haisley, L., Manning, C., & Fein, D. (2015). Can screening with the Ages and Stages Questionnaire detect autism? *Journal of Developmental and Behavioral Pediatrics, 36*, 536–543.

Hart, B., & Risley, T. (1995). *Meaningful differences in the everyday experience of young American children*. Baltimore, MD: Brookes.

Hayiou-Thomas, M. E., Dale, P. S., & Plomin, R. (2012). The etiology of variation in language skills changes with development: A longitudinal twin study of language from 2 to 12 years. *Developmental Science, 15*, 233–249.

Heineman, K. R., Schendelaar, P., Van Den Heuvel, E. R., & Hadders-Algra, M. (2018). Motor development in infancy is related to cognitive function at 4 years of age. *Developmental Medicine and Child Neurology, 60*, 1149–1155.

Hensch, T. K. (2004). Critical period regulation. *Annual Review of Neuroscience, 27*, 549–579.

Hoyme, H. E., Kalberg, W. O., Elliott, A. J., Blankenship, J., et al. (2016). Updated clinical guidelines for diagnosing fetal alcohol spectrum disorders. *Pediatrics, 138*, 1–18.

Hubel, D. H., & Wiesel, T. N. (1970). The period of susceptibility to the physiological effects of unilateral eye closure in kittens. *Journal of Physiology, 206*, 419–436.

Hutchon, B. (2018). Minor neurological dysfunction and other comorbidities in children born extremely preterm. *Developmental Medicine and Child Neurology, 60*, 737.

IDEA. (1997). *Individuals with Disabilities Education Act amendments of 1997, 20 U.S.C. 1431 et seq (Fed. Reg. 34).*

IDEA. (2004). *Individuals With Disabilities Education Improvement Act of 2004, Pub. L, No. 108-446, 118 Stat. 2647.*

Iverson, J. M., & Goldin Meadow, S. (2005). Gesture paves the way for language development. *Psychological Science, 16*, 367–371.

Johnson, M. H., Jones, E. J., & Gliga, T. (2015). Brain adaptation and alternative developmental trajectories. *Development and Psychopathology, 27*, 425–442.

Johnson, S., & Marlow, N. (2017). Early and long-term outcome of infants born extremely preterm. *Archives of Disease in Childhood, 102*, 97–102.

Johnson, C. P., Myers, S. M., & American Academy of Pediatrics Council of Children with Disabilities. (2007). Identification and evaluation of children with autism spectrum disorders. *Pediatrics, 120*, 1183–1215.

Johnson, S. B., Riis, J. L., & Noble, K. G. (2016). State of the art review: Poverty and the developing brain. *Pediatrics, 137*, 1–16.

Johnson, S., Wolke, D., & Marlow, N. (2008). Developmental assessment of preterm infants at 2 years: Validity of parent reports. *Developmental Medicine and Child Neurology, 50*, 58–62.

Joint Committee on Infant Hearing. (2000). JCIH 2000 position statement: Principles and guidelines for early hearing detection and intervention programs. *American Journal of Audiology, 9*, 9–29.

Jusczyk, P. W., Houston, D. M., & Newsome, M. (1999). The beginnings of word segmentation in English-learning infants. *Cognitive Psychology, 39*, 159–207.

Kerr-Wilson, C. O., Mackay, D. F., Smith, G. C. S., & Pell, J. R. (2011). Meta-analysis of the association between preterm delivery and intelligence. *Journal of Public Health, 34*, 209–216.

Keunen, K., Benders, M. J., Leemans, A., Firet Van Stam, D. C., et al. (2017). White matter maturation in the neonatal brain is predictive of school age cognitive capacities in children born very preterm. *Developmental Medicine and Child Neurology, 59*, 939–946.

Klein, S. K., & Rapin, I. (1990). Clinical assessment of pediatric disorders of higher cerebral function. *Current Problems in Pediatrics, 20*, 7–60.

Knopik, V. S., Maccani, M. A., Francazio, S., & McGeary, J. E. (2012). The epigenetics of maternal cigarette smoking during pregnancy and effects on child development. *Development and Psychopathology, 24*, 1377–1390.

Knudsen, E. I. (2004). Sensitive periods in the development of the brain and behavior. *Journal of Cognitive Neuroscience, 16*, 1412–1425.

Kolb, B., & Gibb, R. (2007). Brain plasticity and recovery from early cortical injury. *Developmental Neuropsychology, 49*, 107–118.

Kolb, B., & Gibb, R. (2013). Searching for the principles of brain plasticity and behavior. *Cortex, 58*, 251–260.

Kolb, B., Harker, A., & Gibb, R. (2017). Principles of plasticity in the developing brain. *Developmental Medicine and Child Neurology, 59*, 1218–1223.

Kolb, B., Mychasiuk, R., Williams, P., & Gibb, R. (2011). Brain plasticity and recovery from early cortical injury. *Developmental Medicine and Child Neurology, 53*(Suppl. 4), 4–8.

Kuhl, P. K., Williams, K. A., Lacerda, F., Stevens, K. N., & Lindblom, B. (1992). Linguistic experience alters phonetic perception in infants by 6 months of age. *Science, 255*, 606–608.

Laptook, A. R. (2016). Birth asphyxia and hypoxic-ischemic brain injury in the preterm infant. *Clinics in Perinatology, 43*, 529–545.

Laptook, A. R., Shankaran, S., Tyson, J. E., Munoz, B., Bell, E., Goldberg, R. N., et al. (2017). Effect of therapeutic hypothermia initiated after 6 hours of age on death or disability among newborns with hypoxic-ischemic encephalopathy. *Journal of the American Medical Association, 318*, 1550–1560.

Larson, J. J., Graham, D. L., Singer, L. T., et al. (2019). Cognitive and behavioral impact on children exposed to opioids curing pregnancy. *Pediatrics, 144*, 1–12.

Lemon, R. N. (2008). Descending pathways in motor control. *Annual Review of Neuroscience, 31*, 195–218.

Lenroot, R. K., & Giedd, J. N. (2006). Brain development in children and adolescents: Insight from anatomical magnetic resonance imaging. *Neuroscience and Biobehavioral Reviews*, (6), 718–729.

Leonard, L. B. (2014). Children with specific language impairment and their contribution to the study of language development. *Journal of Child Language*, 38–47.

LeParo, K. M., Justice, L., Skibbe, L. E., & Pianta, R. C. (2004). Relations among maternal, child, and demographic factors and the persistence of preschool language impairment. *American Journal of Speech-Language Pathology, 13*, 291–303.

Lester, B. M., Conradt, E., & Marsit, C. (2016). Introduction to the special section on epigenetics. *Child Development, 87*, 29–37.

Lester, B., Marsit, C., Conradt, E., Bromer, C., & Padbury, J. (2012). Behavioral epigenetics and the developmental origins of mental health disorders. *Journal of Developmental Origins of Health and Disease, 3*, 395–408.

Lipina, S. J., & Posner, M. I. (2012). The impact of poverty on the development of brain networks. *Frontiers in Human Neuroscience, 6*, 238.

Luby, J. L. (2015). Poverty's most insidious damage. The developing brain. *JAMA Pediatrics, 169*, 810–811.

Macy, M., Bagnato, S. J., Macy, R. S., & Salaway, J. (2015). Conventional tests and testing for early identification eligibility. *Infants and Young Children, 28*, 182–204.

Marlow, N., Wolke, D., Bracewell, M. A., & Samara, M. (2005). EPICure Study Group. Neurologic and developmental disability at six years of age after extremely preterm birth. *New England Journal of Medicine, 353*, 9–19.

Martin, J. H., Chakrabarty, S., & Friel, K. M. (2011). Harnessing activity-dependent plasticity to repair the damaged corticospinal tract in an animal model of CP. *Developmental Medicine and Child Neurology*, *53*(Suppl. 4), 9–13.

Martin, A. J., Darlow, B. A., Salt, A., Hague, W., et al. (2013). Performance of the parent report of children's abilities-revised (PARCA-R) versus the Bayley Scales of Infant Development III. *Archives of Disease in Childhood*, (12), 955–958.

McGowan, J. E., Aldirice, F. A., Holmes, V. A., & Johnson, L. (2011). Early childhood development of late-preterm infants: A systematic review. *Pediatrics*, *127*, 1111–1122.

McCall, R. B. (1983). A conceptual approach to early mental development. In M. Lewis (Ed.), *Origins of intelligence: Infancy and early childhood* (pp. 107–134). New York: Plenum.

Menon, V. (2013). Developmental pathways to functional brain networks: Emerging principles. *Trends in Cognitive Sciences*, *17*, 627–640.

Miguel, P. M., Pereira, L. O., Silveira, P. P., & Meany, M. J. (2019). Early environmental influences on the development of children's brain structure and function. *Developmental Medicine and Child Neurology*, *61*, 1127–1133.

Milani-Comparetti, A., & Gidoni, E. A. (1967). Pattern analysis of motor development and its disorders. *Developmental Medicine and Child Neurology*, *9*, 631–636.

Moldavsky, M., Lev, D., & Lerman-Sagie, T. (2001). Behavioral phenotypes of genetic syndromes: A reference guide for psychiatrists. *Journal of the American Academy of Child and Adolescent Psychiatry*, *40*, 749–760.

Morsan, V., Fantoni, C., & Tallandini, M. A. (2018). Age correction in cognitive, linguistic, and motor domains for infants born preterm: An analysis of the Bayley Scales of Infant and Toddler Development Third Edition, developmental patterns. *Developmental Medicine and Child Neurology*, *6*, 820–825.

Mulder, H., Hoofs, H., Verhagen, J., van der Veen, I., & Leseman, P. M. (2014). Psychometric properties and convergent and predictive validity of an executive function test battery for two-year-olds. *Frontiers in Psychology*, *5*, 733–750.

Mulder, H., Pitchford, N. J., & Marlow, N. (2010). Processing speed and working memory underlie academic attainment in very preterm children. *Archives of Disease in Childhood. Fetal and Neonatal Edition*, *95*, F267–F272.

Nazzi, T., & Ramus, R. (2003). Perception and acquisition of linguistic rhythm by infants. *Speech Communication*, *41*, 233–243.

Nemati, F., & Kolb, B. (2010). Motor cortex injury has different behavioral and anatomic effects in juvenile and adolescent rats. *Behavioral Neuroscience*, *24*, 612–622.

Nemati, F., & Kolb, B. (2012). Recovery from medial prefrontal cortex injury during adolescence. Implications for age-dependent plasticity. *Behavioural Brain Research*, *229*, 168–175.

Nigg, J. T. (2018). Toward an emerging paradigm for understanding attention-deficit/hyperactivity disorder and other neurodevelopmental, mental and behavioral disorders. Environmental risks and epigenetic associations. *JAMA Pediatrics*, *172*, 619–621.

Noble, K. G., Houston, S. M., Brio, N. H., et al. (2015). Family income, parental education and brain structure in children and adolescents. *Nature Neuroscience*, *18*, 773–778.

Noritz, G. H., Murphy, N. A., & Neuromotor Screening Expert Panel. (2013). Motor delays: Early identification and evaluation. *Pediatrics*, *131*, e2016–e2027.

Novak, I., Hines, M., Goldsmith, S., & Barclay, R. (2012). Clinical prognostic messages from a systematic review on cerebral palsy. *Pediatrics*, *130*, e1285–e1312.

Novak, I., Morgan, C., McNamara, L., & te Velde, A. (2019). Best practice guidelines for communicating to parents the diagnosis of disability. *Early Human Development*, [in press]. https://doi.org/10.1016/j.earlhumdev.2019.104841.

Novak, I., Spirit Jones, A., & Morgan, C. (2017). First words: Speech and language intervention in cerebral palsy. *Developmental Medicine and Child Neurology*, *59*, 343–344.

Oien, R. A., Schjolberg, S., Volkmar, F. R., Shic, F., Cicchetti, D. V., Nordal-Hansen, A., et al. (2018). Clinical features of children with autism who passed 18-month screening. *Pediatrics*, *141*, 1–10.

Palisano, R., Rosenbaum, P., Bartlett, D., & Livingston, M. H. (2008). Content validity of the expanded and revised Gross Motor Function Classification System. *Developmental Medicine and Child Neurology, 50*, 744–750.

Palisano, R., Rosenbaum, P., Walter, S., Russell, D., Woods, E., & Galuppi, B. (1997). Development and reliability of a system to classify gross motor function in children with cerebral palsy. *Developmental Medicine and Child Neurology, 39*, 214–223.

Paneth, N. (2018). Hypoxia-ischemia and brain injury in infants born preterm. *Developmental Medicine and Child Neurology, 60*, 115.

Parade, S. H., Rodpit, L. L., Seifer, R., Armstrong, D.A., Marsit, C. J., et al. (2016). Methylation of the glucocorticoid receptor gene promotor in preschoolers: Links with internalizing behavior problems. *Child Development, 86*, 303–309.

Parekh, S. A., Boyle, E., Guy, A., Blaggan, S., Manktelow, B. N., Wolke, D., et al. (2016). Correcting for prematurity affects developmental test scores in infants born late and moderately preterm. *Early Human Development, 94*, 1–6.

Parker, S. E., Mai, C. T., Canfield, M. A., Wang, R. R., Meyer, R. E., et al. (2010). Updated national birth prevalence estimates for selected birth defects in the US, 2004–2006. *Birth Defects Research Part A: Clinical and Molecular Teratology, 88*, 1008–1016.

Pelligrino, J. E., & Pelligrino, L. (2008). Fetal alcohol syndrome and related disorders. In P. Accardo (Ed.), *Vol. 1. Capute and Accardo's neurodevelopmental disabilities in infancy and childhood* (pp. 269–283). Baltimore, MD: Paul H. Brookes.

Pena, E. D., Spaulding, T. J., & Plante, E. (2006). The composition of normative groups and diagnostic decision making: Shooting ourselves in the foot. *American Journal of Speech-Language Pathology, 15*, 247–254.

Piaget, J., & Inhelder, B. (1969). *The psychology of the child*. New York: Basic Books.

Pierce, K., Gazestani, V. H., Facon, E., Carter-Barnes, C., et al. (2019). Evaluation of the diagnostic stability of the early autism spectrum disorder phenotype in the general population starting at 12 months. *JAMA Pediatrics*, 173(6), 578–587, e1–e10.

Pragatano, G. P., & Gray, J. A. (2011). Conducting feedback for pediatric neuropsychological assessment. In A. S. Davis (Ed.), *Handbook of pediatric neuropsychology* (pp. 495–499). New York: Springer.

Prechtl, H. F. R. (1980). The optimality concept. *Early Human Development, 4*, 201–205.

Radesky, J. S., Carta, J., & Bair-Merritt, M. (2016). The 30 million word gap. Relevance for pediatrics. *JAMA Pediatrics, 170*, 825–826.

Raz, M., & Beatty, B. R. (2018). Replacing the "word gap" with non-stigmatizing approaches to early literacy and language building. *Pediatrics, 142*(6), e20181992.

Reid, S. M., Carlin, J. B., & Reddihough, D. S. (2011). Classification of topographical pattern of spasticity in cerebral palsy: A registry perspective. *Research in Developmental Disabilities, 32*, 2909–2915.

Rescorla, L. (2011). Late talkers: Do good predictors of outcome exist? *Developmental Disabilities Research Reviews, 17*, 141–150.

Rescorla, L., & Alley, A. (2001). Validation of the language development survey (LDS): A parent report tool for identifying language delay in toddlers. *Journal of Speech, Language and Hearing Research, 44*, 434–445.

Restiffe, A. P., & Gherpelli, J. L. (2005). Comparison of chronological and corrected ages in the gross motor assessment of low-risk preterm infants during the first year of life. *Arquivos de Neuro-Psiquiatria, 64*, 418–425.

Rice, M. I. (2013). *Toward a genetics of language*. New York: Psychology Press.

Ritter, B. C., Nelle, M., Perrig, W., Steinlin, M., & Everts, R. (2013). Executive functions of children born very preterm—Deficit or delay? *European Journal of Pediatrics, 172*, 473–483.

Roberts, R. M., George, W. M., Cole, C., Marshall, P., Ellison, V., & Fabel, H. (2013). The effect of age-correction on IQ scores among school-aged children born preterm. *Australian Journal of Educational and Developmental Psychology, 13*, 1–15.

Roberts, H., & Kennert, B. (2018). Primer on special education. In H. Needelman & B. J. Jackson (Eds.), *Follow-up for NICU graduates* (pp. 283–292). New York: Springer.

Robinson, T. E., & Kolb, B. (1999). Alterations in the morphology of dendrites and dendritic spines in the nucleus accumbens and prefrontal cortex following repeated treatment with amphetamine or cocaine. *European Journal of Neuroscience, 11*, 1598–1604.

Romens, S. E., McDonald, J., Svaren, J., & Pollak, S. D. (2015). Associations between early life stress and gene methylation in children. *Child Development, 86*, 303–309.

Rothbart, M., & Posner, M. (2001). Mechanism and variation in the development of attentional networks. In C. Nelson & M. Luciano (Eds.), *Handbook of developmental cognitive neuroscience* (pp. 353–363). Cambridge, MA: MIT Press.

Rudolph, J. M., & Leonard, L. B. (2016). Early language milestones and specific language impairment. *Journal of Early Intervention, 38*, 41–58.

Rueda, M. R., Posner, M. I., & Rothbart, M. (2005). The development of executive attention: Contributions to the emergence of self-regulation. *Developmental Neuropsychology, 28*, 573–594.

Shonkoff, J. P., & Gardner, A. S. (2012). The lifelong effects of early childhood adversity and toxic stress. *Pediatrics, 129*, e232–e276.

Skellern, C. Y., Rogers, Y., & O'Callaghan, M. J. (2001). A parent-completed developmental questionnaire: Follow-up of ex-premature infants. *Journal of Paediatrics and Child Health, 37*, 125–129.

Smearman, E. L., Almli, L. M., Connely, K. N., et al. (2016). Oxytocin receptor genetic and epigenetic variation: Association with child abuse and adult psychiatric symptoms. *Child Development, 87*, 122–134.

Sparrow, S. S., Cicchetti, D., & Saulnier, C. A. (2016). *Vineland-3 manual*. Bloomington, MN: Pearson.

Spitz, R. A. (1945). Hospitalism. *Psychoanalytic Study of the Child, 1*, 53–74.

Tan, C. H., Denny, C. H., Cheal, N. E., Sniezek, J. E., & Kanny, D. (2012). Alcohol use and binge drinking among women of childbearing age—United States, 2011-2013. CDC *MMWR Morbidity and Mortality Weekly Report, 61*, 534–538.

Tan, C. H., Denny, C. H., Cheal, N. E., Sniezek, J. E., & Kanny, D. (2015). Alcohol use and binge drinking among women of childbearing age. *Morbidity and Mortality Weekly Report (MMWR), 64*, 1042–1046.

Tanis-LeMonde, C. S., Bornstein, M. H., & Baumwell, L. (2001). Maternal responsiveness and children's achievement of language milestones. *Child Development, 72*, 748–767.

Taylor, H. G., & Clark, C. A. (2016). Executive function in children born preterm: Risk factors and implications for outcome. *Seminars in Perinatology, 40*, 520–529.

Thurlow, M. L., Elliott, J. E., & Ysseldyke, J. E. (2003). *Testing students with disabilities. Practical strategies for complying with district and state requirements* (2nd ed.). Thousand Oaks, CA: Corwin.

Tomasello, M. (2000). The item-based nature of children's early syntactic development. *Trends in Cognitive Sciences, 4*, 156–163.

Tomblin, J. B., Smith, E., & Zhang, X. (1997). Epidemiology of specific language impairment: Prenatal and perinatal risk factors. *Journal of Communication Disorders, 30*, 325–343.

Tsybina, I., & Eriks-Brophy, A. (2007). Issues in research on children with early language delay. *Contemporary Issues in Communicaton Science and Disorders, 34*, 118–133.

Turk-Brown, N. B., Scholl, B. J., & Chun, M. M. (2008). Babies and brains: Habituation in infant cognition and functional neuroimaging. *Frontiers in Human Neuroscience, 2*(16), 1–11.

Twilhaar, E. S., Wade, R. M., de Kieviet, J. F., et al. (2018). Cognitive outcomes of children born extremely or very preterm since the 1990s and associated risk factors. *JAMA Pediatrics, 172*, 361–367.

Van Houdt, C. A., Oosterlaan, J., Van Wassnaer-Leemhuis, A. G., Van Kaam, A. H., & Aarmpidse-Moens, C. S. (2019). Executive function deficits in children born preterm or at low birthweight: A meta-analysis. *Developmental Medicine and Child Neurology, 61*, 1015–1024.

van Veen, S., Aarnoudse-Moens, C. S. H., van Kaam, A. H., Oosterlaan, J., & van Wassenaer-Leemhuis, A. G. (2016). Consequences of correcting intelligence quotient for prematurity at age 5 years. *Journal of Pediatrics, 173*, 90–95.

Veldhuizen, S., Rodriguez, C., Wade, T. I., & Cairney, I. (2015). Misclassification due to age grouping in measures of child development. *Archives of Disease in Childhood, 100*, 220–224.

Veldman, S. L., Santos, R., Jones, R. A., Sousa-Sa, E., & Okely, A. D. (2019). Associations between gross motor skills and cognitive development in toddlers. *Early Human Development, 132*, 39–44.

Visser, L., Ruiter, S. A., van der Meulen, B. F., Ruijssenaars, W. A., & Timmerman, M. E. (2013). Validity and suitability of the Bayley-III low motor/vision version: A comparative study among young children with and without motor and/or visual impairments. *Research in Developmental Disabilities, 34*, 3736–3745.

Visser, L., Ruiter, S. A., van der Meulen, B. F., Ruijssenaars, W. A., & Timmerman, M. E. (2014). Accommodating the Bayley-III for motor and/or visual impairment. A comparative pilot study. *Pediatric Physical Therapy, 26*, 57–67.

Vohr, B. (2014). Speech and language outcomes of preterm infants. *Seminars in Fetal and Neonatal Medicine, 19*, 78–83.

Vohr, B. R., Stephens, B. E., Higgins, R. D., et al. (2012). The NICHD Neonatal Research Network. Are outcomes of extremely preterm infants improving? Impact of Bayley assessment on outcomes. *Journal of Pediatrics, 161*, 222–228.

Volkow, N. D. (2013). Impact of fetal drug exposures on the adolescent brain. *JAMA Pediatrics, 167*, 390–391.

Volpe, J. J. (2009). Brain injury in premature infants: A complex amalgam of destructive and developmental disturbances. *Lancet Neurology, 8*, 110–124.

Wallace, I. F., Berkman, N. D., Watson, C. R., et al. USPSTF (2015). Screening for speech and language delay in children 5 years old and younger: A systematic review. *Pediatrics, 135*(1–15), Si–S128.

Wetherby, A. M., Woods, J., Allen, L., Cleary, J., Dickinson, H., & Lord, C. (2004). Early indicators of autism spectrum disorders in the second year of life. *Journal of Autism and Developmental Disorders, 34*, 473–493.

Wiebe, S. A., Espy, K. A., & Charak, D. (2008). Using confirmatory factor analysis to understand executive control in preschool children I. Latent structure. *Developmental Psychology, 44*, 575–587.

Wiebe, S. A., Sheffield, T., Nelson, J. M., Clark, C. A. C., Chevalier, N., & Espy, K. A. (2011). The structure of executive function in 3-year-olds. *Journal of Experimental Child Psychology, 108*, 436–452.

Wiggins, L. D., Piazza, V., & Robins, D. L. (2014). Comparison of broad-based screen versus disorder-specific screen in detecting young children with autism spectrum disorder. *Autism, 18*, 76–84.

Willett, S. (2018). Developmental care in the nursery. In H. Needelman & B. J. Jackson (Eds.), *Follow-up for NICU graduates. Promoting positive developmental and behavioral outcomes for at-risk infants* (pp. 15–58). New York: Springer.

Wilson, S. L., & Cradock, M. M. (2004). Review: Accounting for prematurity in developmental assessment and the use of age-adjusted scores. *Journal of Pediatric Psychology, 29*, 641–649.

Wilson, P. H., Ruddock, S., Smits-Engelsman, B., Polatajko, I. T., & Blank, R. (2013). Understanding performance deficits in developmental coordination disorder: A meta-analysis of recent research. *Developmental Medicine and Child Neurology, 16*, 573–581.

Wilson-Ching, M., Pascoe, L., Doyle, L. W., & Anderson, P. J. (2014). Effects of correcting for prematurity on cognitive test scores in childhood. *Journal of Paediatrics and Child Health, 50*, 182–188.

Wolraich, M. L., Felice, M. E., & Drotar, D. (Eds.), (1996). *The classification of child and adolescent mental diagnosis in primary care: Diagnosis and Statistical Manual for Primary Care (DSM-PC). Child and adolescent version.* Elk Grove, IL: American Academy of Pediatrics.

Woodbury-Smith, M., & Scherer, S. (2018). Progress in the genetics of autism spectrum disorder. *Developmental Medicine and Child Neurology*, *60*, 445–451.

Xu, G., Strathearn, L., Liu, B., O'Brien, M., Kopelman, T. G., Zhu, J., et al. (2018). Prevalence and treatment patterns of autism spectrum disorder in the United States. *JAMA Pediatrics*, *173*, 153–159.

Yuen, T., Penner, M., Carter, M. T., & Szatmari, P. K. (2018). Assessing the accuracy of the Modified Checklist for Autism in Toddlers: A systematic review and meta-analysis. *Developmental Medicine and Child Neurology*, *60*, 1093–1100.

Zablotsky, B., Black, L. I., Maenner, M. J., & Schieve, L. A. (2015). Estimated prevalence of autism and other developmental disabilities following questionnaire changes in the 2014 DHHS National Health Interview Survey. *National Health Statistics Reports*, *87*, 1–20.

Zhu, J., & Chen, H. (2011). Utility of inferential norming with smaller sample sizes. *Journal of Psychoeducational Assessment*, *29*, 570–580.

Zimmerman, I. L., Steiner, V. G., & Pond, R. E. (2002). *Preschool language scale* (4th ed.). San Antonio, TX: The Psychological Corporation.

Zwaigenbaum, L., Bauman, M. L., Fein, D., Pierce, K., Buie, T., et al. (2015). Early screening of autism spectrum disorder: Recommendations for practice and research. *Pediatrics*, *136*, 541–559.

Zwicker, J. G., Missiuna, C., Harris, S. R., & Boyd, L. A. (2012). Developmental coordination disorder a review and update. *European Journal of Paediatric Neurology*, *16*, 573–581.

Index

Note: Page numbers followed by *f* indicate figures.

C

D